THE GLORIOUS CHURCH

RECOMMENDATIONS

Jesus loves the Church, and He has a great plan for His Church. This book will include you in that plan by guiding you through Bible stories and personal experiences and make you taste the passion for God's dream: a church full of love for Jesus that makes an impact on the world around it. Highly recommended for every believer who has a desire to work with God's plan in these times.

~Peter Paauwe – Senior Pastor DoorBrekers

Since the COVID-19 crisis, the church structure as we know it, which was comfortable for many people, has been under pressure because it was a "consumption model" where visitors get presented with a nice message and a worship session. However, God does not want us to be consumers. God wants us to be producers that carry much fruit in His Kingdom (John 15:8). God wants to reset the church from a consumer model to a producer model, and Ben Kroeske has been excellently successful in changing the perspective that many people in the Netherlands have on the Church with this book. Let the teaching deeply impact you, change your perspective of the church, and be a powerful producer in the Kingdom of God. This book will give you specific tools to be a part of the Church that Jesus intends to have without spot or wrinkle. Together, we form the Church in the Netherlands, and together, we can be the Church as Christ intended her to be.

~Tom de Wal – Founder Frontrunners Ministries

Thankful for this new book out of the hands of Ben Kroeske on this so important topic in which few believers really see God's vision: the church.

God's focus at the start was to establish a family full of Himself, full of glory, love, truth, and His representation on earth (Gen. 1:27-28). We can see through the whole Word of God representatives and messengers of this glory, but the real carrier of the glory of God is the church!

Be inspired by this book to see the church as Jesus sees it, become part of it and in UNITY, honor our Savior and IN HIS NAME, win and disciple precious souls!

God's loving blessing while reading,

~**Arno van der Knaap – Lead Pastor GOD Centre**

THE GLORIOUS CHURCH

BEN KROESKE

Without limiting the rights under copyright(s) reserved below, no part of this publication may be reproduced, stored in, or introduced into a retrieval system or transmitted in any form or by any means (electronic, mechanical, photocopying, recording, or otherwise) without the prior permission of the publisher and the copyright owner.

The content of this book is provided "AS IS." The publisher and the author make no guarantees or warranties as to the accuracy, adequacy, or completeness of or results to be obtained from using the content of this book, including any information that can be accessed through hyperlinks or otherwise, and expressly disclaim any warranty expressed or implied, including but not limited to implied warranties of merchantability or fitness for a particular purpose. This limitation of liability shall apply to any claim or cause whatsoever, whether such claim or cause arises in contract, tort, or otherwise. In short, you, the reader, are responsible for your choices and the results they bring.

The scanning, uploading, and distributing of this book via the internet or any other means without the permission of the publisher and copyright owner is illegal and punishable by law. Please purchase only authorized copies, and do not participate in or encourage piracy of copyrighted materials. Your support of the author's rights is appreciated.

Unless otherwise indicated, Scriptures are taken from the NEW KING JAMES VERSION : Scripture taken from the NEW KING JAMES VERSION®. Copyright© 1982 by Thomas Nelson, Inc. Used by permission. All rights reserved.

Copyright © 2024 by Ben Kroeske. All rights reserved.

Released February 2024
ISBN: 978-1-64457-714-1

Rise UP Publications
644 Shrewsbury Commons Ave
Ste 249
Shrewsbury PA 17361
United States of America
www.riseUPpublications.com
Phone: 866-846-5123

CONTENTS

Introduction	9
CHAPTER 1	15
A Church full of glory	
What is God's Glory?	18
The Body Filled with Glory	27
Looking Back at David	28
The Desire for the Glory	31
A Dead-End Road	32
Brought to a Standstill	36
The Road from God to the Glory	38
Experience with God's Glory	40
CHAPTER 2	43
The Glorious Church Shines!	
The Great Commission	48
Covered	50
CHAPTER 3	61
The Glorious Church Radiates	
Holy and Spotless	62
Fire Makes You Pure	67
Fire Now or Fire Later	69
A Church Full of the Holy Spirit!	71
The Promise Fulfilled!	73
A Reflection of His Glory	76
CHAPTER 4	79
The Glorious Church Is United	
Spiritual Gifts Are Not a Sign of Spiritual Maturity	81
The Glorious Church Is in Unison	83
Jan Sjoerd Pasterkamp	84
We Break the Force of Division by Embracing a Culture of Honor	86
A Culture of Honor	88

CHAPTER 5   95
The Glorious Church Overcomes

Afterword   109
About the Author   119
About the River Amsterdam   121
About River Bible Institute   123

INTRODUCTION

From the foundation of the world, God wanted a family. He wanted mature sons and daughters with His DNA who would be a reflection of His glory. He longs for so much more than a group of people who come together in a building. He longs for more than an organization, more than programs and great events. His passionate desire is a powerful and living Body, of which He is the head.

God dreamt of living stones put together to create a beautiful temple. He dreamt of a resting place for Himself where He could enjoy his own creation as He intended her to be. A utopian thought? For a cynical humanity, it probably is, but not for God's children who know His heart. Our God and Father is a Dreamer and a Visionary. He is the Alpha and Omega, the Master Strategist who already sees the end at the beginning. He is both the Architect Who created the plans and the Master Builder of His own dream house. What a privilege to be part of the temple where God lives.

When I gave my life to Jesus in 2006, love for the Church also streamed into my heart at that moment. I wrote this book because it is my desire to bring across some of the passion that God has laid in me for His Bride, the Church. When you talk to people about "church," you often receive negative reactions. The criticism comes from different places. A lot of Western people have no interest in the topic of "church." They live their lives and often have a negative view of "the church." The negative reactions sometimes come from Christians who have become disappointed for whichever reason and choose to no longer be dedicated to a local church. Finally, there also is a group that is faithful to tradition and goes to the services of a local church, but a real passion for God or the Church is out of the question.

I believe with my whole heart that God did not want it this way, and it is possible to do things very differently. I believe that if you are part of a local church...

- where the Holy Spirit is tangibly present,
- where the love for each other becomes visible,
- where new people constantly come in,
- where in every meeting, people are saved, healed, and delivered,
- where lives are visibly transformed,
- that it will be a great joy to be part of that church.

This book is not an attempt to draw a picture of a perfect local church because we all know that a church like that does not exist. God is diverse and multi-colored, which means that every local church is also allowed to have its own color. This book is mainly about the church with a capital C, the Church that the Lord is building passionately. I believe the signs of the end times are becoming more and more visible at a rapid pace and that Jesus is coming back soon to get His Bride. This is why I felt an urgency to write this book and why I am joining in building the glorious Church day in and day out—the one He is coming back for.

This book will challenge and encourage you to be part of that glorious Church in all her facets. How great it is to be part of that end-time Church. We have the enormous privilege to be allowed to be carriers of His presence and to make a difference in our current world in the name of Jesus before He comes back.

He wants the Church to stand radiating before Him, perfect, without spot or wrinkle. I believe He is coming back for a Bride that is holy and pure. A Bride that eagerly awaits the coming of the heavenly Bridegroom.

> *That He might present her to Himself a glorious church, not having spot or wrinkle or any such thing, but that she should be holy and without blemish.*
>
> — EPHESIANS 5:27

Before I started writing this book, I had a period of fasting and prayer. I had set this time apart to pray for the local church that my wife and I lead. The Lord encouraged me to write down the vision He laid on my heart for our local church in bullet points. I believe this vision is not just for the River Amsterdam but that there are many people in the Netherlands walking around with the same desire in their hearts. I am sharing the vision here, hoping it will resound in your heart.

The church I see…

- A church so full of dynamic praise that an atmosphere of great joy is set free.
- A church so deep in intimate worship that it attracts the glory of God.
- A church so filled with the presence of God that everyone who comes in tastes a piece of heaven and gets marked by a realization of eternity.
- A church where the Word is preached uncompromised so that people grow into Christ as strong disciples. A place where a new generation of leaders is being raised and equipped to make an impact on this earth.
- A church that beams out the gospel message through every form of media so the world gets the chance to know Jesus.
- A church where people give their lives to Jesus every week, find forgiveness for their sins and are delivered from all guilt and shame.
- A church where the Holy Spirit can freely move and touch people. A church where people do not just hear about God but where they truly experience Him.
- A church without selfish ambition or division but where the Holy Spirit forges people together into true unity.
- A church with a true heart to serve Christ both inside and outside the walls of the church building and to show His humble heart by reaching out to the less fortunate in this world.
- A generous church that impacts the world and lays up heavenly treasures by generously supporting projects that are initiated by God with financial resources.

- A church with a passion for lost souls and broken people so that every day, people are ripped out of the kingdom of darkness and become part of the kingdom of God.
- A church where people with different backgrounds, cultures, races, and statuses find a home where they can grow and flourish in their walk with Christ, discover their purpose, and learn to walk it out.
- This church is a center of revival for the nation. A place from which people can be sent out into the nations of this world. A training center for the next generation. This church is the River Amsterdam, and this church is YOU!

Ben Kroeske

1

A CHURCH FULL OF GLORY

'The glory of this latter temple shall be greater than the former,' says the Lord of hosts.

— HAGGAI 2:9

David was a successful king who reigned over Israel from Jerusalem. God had given him victory over all his enemies, and after much warfare and struggle, everything in his life seemed to be smooth sailing. Yet, there was something that was nagging at David's heart. It bothered him that he was living in a beautiful palace while the ark of God stood in a tent. In that time, the ark represented God's presence on earth as a foreshadowing of Jesus, who would be coming later. The thought would not leave him, and the desire to build a house for God became stronger and stronger. He discussed this desire with the prophet Nathan, and without consulting the Lord, Nathan said, "Go ahead and do whatever you have in mind, for the Lord is with you." However, that night, Nathan received a word from the Lord for David, "Are you the one to build a house for Me to live in?" The Lord continued on, and His words, in short, come down to this, "I have moved around with the Israelites in a tent, and have I ever asked them to build a house for Me?" God then points out to David that He took him away from the flock of his father to become king instead of Saul and that He worked out David's kingship by giving him rest from all his enemies. Finally, God makes a statement, "I will build you a house." David did not understand those words, nor the rest of the words God spoke through the prophet Nathan:

> *When your days are fulfilled and you rest with your fathers, I will set up your seed after you, who will come from your body, and I will establish his kingdom. He shall build a house for My name, and I will establish the throne of his kingdom forever. I will be his Father, and he shall be My son.*
>
> — 2 SAMUEL 7:12-14

God said to David, "Not you, but someone from your offspring will build a house for My glory." As New Testament Christians, we know that God spoke about the coming Messiah here. One day in the future, Jesus would come, and He would build a house for God's name. This would not be an earthly building but a spiritual Body built with living stones. God spoke about the Church, a people in which He would live in, and that would be set apart to proclaim His mighty deeds.

David did not understand the meaning of those words. He thought Solomon was the designated person to build a temple after his death for the glory of God. It had to be a beautiful building where people from all over the world could come to worship the God of Israel.

When Solomon was done building this magnificent temple, he called the elders and all the leaders of Israel together to consecrate the temple with a feast. The Levites moved the ark out of the tent that his father, David, had set up for the ark. With the carrying poles on their shoulders, they brought the ark to the temple and placed it in the Most Holy Place. The tent itself and all the holy objects that stood in it were also carried into the temple by the priests. When they came outside, an enormous sound of praise erupted. The musicians started a song, and the singers sang a song in unison about the goodness of God while a hundred and twenty priests blew the trumpet. Praise and worship filled the atmosphere when they praised God in unity for His goodness and grace. Together with the sound of the hundred and twenty priests who blew the trumpets, heaven opened over that place. Later, on Pentecost, the same thing happened when a hundred and twenty people in the upper room were waiting on the Holy Spirit, but more on that later!

> *Indeed it came to pass, when the trumpeters and singers were as one, to make one sound to be heard in praising and thanking the Lord, and when they lifted up their voice with the trumpets and cymbals and instruments of music, and praised the Lord, saying:*
> *"For He is good, For His mercy endures forever," that the house, the house of the Lord, was filled with a cloud, so that the priests could not continue ministering because of the*

> *cloud; for the glory of the Lord filled the house of God.*
>
> — 2 CHRONICLES 5:13-14

We read here that God's response came in the form of His glory that became tangibly present in that place. His glory filled the temple. The glory of God was so strong that the priests could not even remain standing! Sometimes, we get visitors in our meetings who ask, "Why do people fall over when you pray for them?" The answer is simple: "Because they no longer could stand!" That is what happens when the supernatural power of God comes into contact with our natural body.

What is God's Glory?

It is His Person in tangible manifestation. It is God who shows Himself in His majesty. The Hebrew word for glory is "kabod." When you translate it literally, it means "weight." The glory is the WEIGHT (kabod) of His Person, the heaviness of His being.

"God does not act like He is weighty. HE IS WEIGHTY!"

That is the reason the priests could no longer stand: the weight of His glory fell on them. The earthly cannot contain the heavenly. That has not changed!

So, the temple of Solomon was filled with the glory of God. Later, when Israel turned against God and went after other gods, the temple was destroyed by enemy armies, and the people were exiled to Babylon. After seventy years of exile, God had mercy on His people, and they could go back to their own country, as He had promised them. After their return, they started rebuilding the temple after God encouraged them through the prophet Haggai to do so. Under the leadership of Zerubbabel, governor of Judah, and Joshua, the high priest, they tenaciously rebuilt the temple in a short period. The temple looked nowhere near as glorious as the temple that Solomon built in his time, but God sent the prophet Haggai again, not to correct them this time, but to encourage them with the following words:

> *"For thus says the Lord of hosts: 'Once more (it is a little while) I will shake heaven and earth, the sea and dry land; and I will shake all nations, and they shall come to the Desire of All Nations, and I will fill this temple with glory,' says the Lord of hosts. 'The silver is Mine, and the gold is Mine,' says the Lord of hosts. 'The glory of this latter temple shall be greater than the former,' says the Lord of hosts. 'And in this place I will give peace,' says the Lord of hosts."*
>
> — HAGGAI 2:6-9

"The latter glory of this house shall be greater than the former!"

God had more glory in store. Maybe you are asking yourself if this prophecy is talking about the temple they just rebuilt. Did this word get fulfilled in that time? The answer to that is "no"! The temple that was rebuilt under the leadership of Zerubbabel and Joshua did not get filled with God's glory. Otherwise, the Holy Spirit would have stated it. God spoke through Haggai not about the earthly temple they rebuilt but about a spiritual temple that would rise up in the future. He prophesied over the body of Jesus. Later, Jesus Himself speaks about His earthly body as a temple. Right before Pascha, He chased all of the sellers of sacrifice animals and money-changers out of the temple with a whip. The Jews were livid and asked Him what right He had to do that, "What sign do you show us for doing these things?" Jesus gave them an answer they understood nothing of, "Destroy this temple, and in three days I will raise it up." They did not understand that He was speaking about the temple of His body. Jesus was essentially prophesying about His death and resurrection (John 2:13-21). The temple of His body had a much greater glory than any earthly building, and that temple would rise from the dead.

> *"Destroy this temple, and in three days I will raise it up."*
>
> —JOHN 2:19

When Jesus rose from the grave, He rose in glory! With that glorified body, He went back to the Father after He had given His disciples the command to wait in Jerusalem for the fulfillment of the promise regarding the Holy Spirit. We, as believers, now form His body here on earth. We are the latter temple that is filled with greater glory! The earthly building was never on God's agenda. It was always about Jesus and His Body, the Church.

The promise of greater glory was fulfilled in Acts 2 during the outpouring of the Holy Spirit.

> *When the Day of Pentecost had fully come, they were all with one accord in one place. And suddenly there came a sound from heaven, as of a rushing mighty wind, and it filled the whole house where they were sitting. Then there appeared to them divided tongues, as of fire, and one sat upon each of them. And they were all filled with the Holy Spirit and began to speak with other tongues, as the Spirit gave them utterance.*
>
> — ACTS 2:1-4

When a crowd from the city heard the sound, they came to see what was happening in that upper room. Peter stood up and began to preach with the following words, inspired by the Holy Spirit.

> *But Peter, standing up with the eleven, raised his voice and said to them, "Men of Judea and all who dwell in Jerusalem, let this be known to you, and heed my words. For these are not drunk, as you suppose, since it is only the third hour of the day. But this is what was spoken by the prophet Joel:* **'And it shall come to pass in the last days, says God, That I will pour out of My Spirit on all flesh;** *Your sons and your daughters shall prophesy, Your young men shall see visions, Your old men shall dream dreams. And on My*

> *menservants and on My maidservants I will pour out My Spirit in those days; And they shall prophesy.*
>
> — ACTS 2:14-18

The greater glory had come! Not on a building but on the body of Christ! What riches we have within us and what a great immeasurable treasure is in our earthly vessel. That truly is the essence of His being, and the weight of His Person is poured out in and on us. That is why when Jesus died on the cross, the veil of the temple was torn from top to bottom. This veil hung between the Holy Place and the Most Holy Place, separating God's presence from the people. In this way, God was among them but not accessible to the common man. Only the High Priest was allowed to enter into the Most Holy Place once per year to make atonement for the sins of the people. That veil, a curtain of 10 cm thick, was torn from top to bottom when Jesus breathed His last breath. From that moment on, God's Spirit no longer lived in that earthly building, but He came to live in the hearts of the born-again sons and daughters of God.

"Everything changes when God Himself walks in!"

A few years ago, the beautiful Dutch song "Fill this house with your glory" became extremely popular among Christian circles. We sang the song often during our meetings, and even now, the song is pulled out sometimes. It is a beautiful song, but there is a danger that we miss what it really is about. We miss the point if we unconsciously long for a physical cloud that fills our place of coming together. The Old Covenant, however, only gives a foreshadowing of the reality of the New Covenant in which we live.

Many Christians want something visible: a cloud, an angel, or a pillar of fire. They read about the cloud of glory that filled the temple and want that cloud to become visible in the meeting. It is not impossible that we see that happen, but it does not have to be our focus. We need to understand that IN JESUS, the fullness of the Godhead lives bodily. We need to keep our eyes on Jesus! He is the Image of the invisible God. He is the glorification of God revealed. He came into the world with "a glory as of the only Son from the Father," and the Father witnessed of Him, "This is my beloved Son, listen to him!"

Sometimes, we have the tendency to find a Jesus+ gospel. Jesus plus an experience, Jesus plus a theory, Jesus plus a revelation, but actually, everything points to Jesus, and everything is about Jesus. Everything in our being Christian should revolve around Jesus. He is The central figure in the history of the universe. We even count our years in the years before Christ and the years after Christ. Let us not forget that the Holy Spirit, who came to fill the church with the glory of God, also bears witness to Jesus. He takes everything from Jesus and reveals it to us. His goal is always to lift Jesus up.

The illustration we see in 2 Chronicles 5 is a foreshadowing of what took place in Acts 2. There, not only the building was filled, but most importantly, the Body. The believers were submerged in the Holy Spirit, filled with glory, and immersed with power. From that day, revival broke out, first in Jerusalem, but from there, the fire of revival went through the whole of Asia Minor and further in a short period. The glorious Church became visible! Even so much visible that it was being said, "The people who came to set the world upside down have also come here!"

Let us put ourselves in the shoes of Philip and try to envision everything he experienced. Maybe he was there on the day of Pentecost. We, of course, do not know, but just imagine…

All of a sudden, there is that noise of an overwhelming stormy wind out of heaven, and the deafening sound fills the house where you have been waiting for the fulfillment of the promise with the other disciples for ten days already. The Holy Spirit would come; that was what Jesus promised. In the past few days, there have been many conversations about how that would be, but nobody seemed to know exactly. All different types of scenarios came by, but this… no, nobody could have thought of this. It is overwhelming; words fail, everyone seems speechless, and it is like time is standing still. Your eyes register the sea of fire in which you have ended up, but the glory of God is filling your entire being in that same moment. Words are streaming from your lips; you can hear them, but you do not recognize the language you are speaking. It does not matter; an indescribable joy fills your heart. His presence is in you. Rivers of living water look for a way out in words you do not understand yourself, but the people start to cry and call out to God. Thousands of people come to Jesus.

Jesus had spoken about it: The Holy Spirit is WITH you, but He will be IN you!

You were there when Jesus stood up during the Feast of Tabernacles to prophesy about the outpouring of the Holy Spirit, "Out of your heart will flow rivers of living water!" (John 7:38).

Now, you are experiencing it yourself! What a joy and what a glory! So many times in your life, you have thirsted for God and wanted to know Him! Every time, you tried your best to keep the rules, made the necessary offers, and please God in every possible way. But it left you empty every time. Religion could not quench the thirst!

Then, just live a little looser, taste a little of a world without God... the kick was always only short, the shame endlessly longer.

But now, this is it. Everything is different! Never have you dared to dream that something like this would happen. Your thirst has been quenched, the emptiness filled, the shame over, and the chains broken. You experience a euphoric feeling of fulfillment and freedom. You know deep inside: Never will I thirst for anything else. I am full, more than full!

For days and weeks after, you are pinching yourself regularly. Did this really happen? All of Jerusalem is turned upside down because of the movement of the Holy Spirit, and you are in the midst of it.

You get chosen to help the apostles; you are allowed to serve the tables for the food program that has started. The apostles lay hands on you and six other men for that important task.

New people are giving their lives to Jesus daily; it is impossible to keep up. You're working side by side with Stephen, who is not only serving the tables but also doing mighty miracles among the people. He is your friend, and you also gradually become bolder in stepping out. The shock is great when your good friend is stoned because of his faith, and persecution breaks out against the Church.

Many followers of Jesus leave the city, and since you could be the next target, you also decide to leave. You move to the city of Samaria but do not want to keep your mouth closed about Jesus, and you cannot. Also, in these intense times, it is brewing inside you—the source of joy and power in you and the living water that wants to flow.

You witness of Jesus; how can you keep your mouth closed? You are preaching the good news to anyone who wants to listen, and to your great joy, many people are healed and delivered. The town is already filled with the Word of the Gospel very quickly. Thousands of people are giving their lives to Jesus and are baptized, and God is using you! Demons flee on your command, and the lame jump up when you pray the prayer of faith for them.

Samaria is turned upside down, and the apostles in Jerusalem hear the good reports. Peter and John are sent to come and help.

Those men carry a weight in God that you do not have yet. When they pray for the new believers, they are all filled with the Holy Spirit. You realize that the scenario in Jerusalem is repeating itself here: crowds are giving their lives to Jesus, they are filled with the Holy Spirit, and they are starting to flood their world with the good news. This movement is unstoppable! It is not by the works of man; this is the work of the Holy Spirit!

God HIMSELF is building His Church. God HIMSELF attracts the crowds towards Him. God HIMSELF is speaking through you and convinces the listeners. It is the hand of the Lord; you are just the glove! You move along while He is doing His work through you!

Does this illustration of Acts form the pinnacle of the Church of Jesus Christ? Is it a beautiful time to look back on and talk about, but not something we can expect today? Absolutely not! When a baby is born, it has all the limbs, But if everything is alright, all those limbs grow, and the muscles become stronger as the child becomes an adult. Would the Lord not give a large wave of grace before His return, in which the crowds of the world get the chance to still give their life to this wonderful Savior before He comes to judge the world? We know from the Word that God does not want even one person to be lost, but He longs that every person comes to repentance. As a Man of the field, He patiently waits until the early and late rain has fallen on the earth and the harvest is ripe. Knowing Him, we can expect that He still has a mighty move of the Holy Spirit in store for us so that a large harvest will be brought in before His coming.

The Body Filled with Glory

The New Testament clearly shows that all born-again Christians form the Body of Christ together. We are the Body of Christ, and separately, we are members of that same Body. We are not members of a church community or denomination, but in the first place, we are members of the Body of Christ. Of course, being part of a local church and serving God together is important. But we will get back to that in a later chapter. Firstly, it is important to establish that we, as the worldwide Body of Christ, are the temple He wants to fill with His glory.

> *Now you are the body of Christ, and members individually.*
>
> — 1 CORINTHIANS 12:27

> *For you are the temple of the living God.*
>
> — 2 CORINTHIANS 6:16

What if God wants to give the Church a movement that will touch the entire world? What if we live in a time now in which God wants to shake all the nations until a great awakening takes place? I believe that this is the best hour for the Church. Whatever is happening on the world stage, either in politics, on the economic level, or in any area, the Church will triumph! Jesus has saved the best for last for us, His Bride. He showed us through His first miracle in the wedding at Cana, where He changed water into wine. He saved the best wine for last!

> *For if the ministry of condemnation had glory,*
> *the ministry of righteousness exceeds much*
> *more in glory.*
>
> — 2 CORINTHIANS 3:9

"Let us hunger more than ever for that glory!"

Looking Back at David

At this point, I want to go back with you to the story of King David. At the beginning of this chapter, we read how David longed to build a temple for the ark, the temple that eventually was built by his son Solomon. We will go back further in time now because when David conquered Jerusalem and made the city the center of government, the ark was not there yet. But where was it then?

For a long time, the ark stood in Kiriath-jearim, in the house of Abinadab. You can read how the ark got there in the first book of Samuel in chapters 1 to 7. We get to know the priest Eli, his corrupt sons, and the little Samuel, who grows to be a prophet. The whole story mainly takes place in Shiloh, where the ark stood in the tabernacle of God. The people of Israel had entered into battle with the Philistines, but when they lost the first battle, they decided to take the ark out of the tabernacle in Shiloh. They thought to be sure of victory in that way, but unfortunately, they were mercilessly conquered by the Philistines, who took the ark back home with them. When the news got to Eli, the priest, he died on the spot. His corrupt sons were killed in the battle, and his daughter-in-law suddenly started having contractions when she heard that her husband was dead. After the birth of her son, she just lived long enough to give her son the name Ichabod, which means: "The glory is gone." As mentioned before, the ark symbolized the glorious presence of God in their midst for the people of Israel. To make a long story short, the Philistines did not know how fast they could return the ark to Israel, where the ark found its home in the house of Abinadab. The ark stood there for a long time as if it was a forgotten symbol of forgotten glory, but David was different than anyone else. David longed to bring the ark to Jerusalem. He wanted to have the glory of God there, close to him in the city where he lived and from which he reigned. In the Bible passage below, we read about how the first attempt of David failed and his eventual success:

> *Then David again gathered all the elite troops in Israel, 30,000 in all. He led them to Baalah of Judah to bring back the Ark of God, which bears the name of the Lord of Heaven's Armies, who is enthroned between the cherubim. They placed the Ark of God on a new cart and brought it from Abinadab's house, which was on a hill. Uzzah and Ahio, Abinadab's sons, were guiding the cart that carried the Ark of God. Ahio walked in front of the Ark. David and all the people of Israel were celebrating before the Lord, singing songs and playing all kinds of musical instruments—lyres, harps, tambourines, castanets, and cymbals.*
> *But when they arrived at the threshing floor of*

Nacon, the oxen stumbled, and Uzzah reached out his hand and steadied the Ark of God. Then the Lord's anger was aroused against Uzzah, and God struck him dead because of this. So Uzzah died right there beside the Ark of God.

David was angry because the Lord's anger had burst out against Uzzah. He named that place Perez-uzzah (which means "to burst out against Uzzah"), as it is still called today.

David was now afraid of the Lord, and he asked, "How can I ever bring the Ark of the Lord back into my care?" So David decided not to move the Ark of the Lord into the City of David. Instead, he took it to the house of Obed-edom of Gath. The Ark of the Lord remained there in Obed-edom's house for three months, and the Lord blessed Obed-edom and his entire household.

Then King David was told, "The Lord has blessed Obed-edom's household and everything he has because of the Ark of God." So David went there and brought the Ark of God from the house of Obed-edom to the City of David with a great celebration. After the men who were carrying the Ark of the Lord had gone six steps, David sacrificed a bull and a fattened calf. And David danced before the Lord with all his might, wearing a priestly garment. So, David and all the people of

> *Israel brought up the Ark of the Lord with*
> *shouts of joy and the blowing of rams' horns.*
>
> — 2 SAMUEL 6:1-15 NLT

Now that we have read it, I want to zoom in on the deeper meaning of this history and the lessons we can learn from it.

The Desire for the Glory

As we can see, the ark is an image of God's glory. David wanted that glory in his life and passionately desired it. His life had been eventful since the day that the prophet Samuel anointed him as the new king of Israel. After being in favor of King Saul for a short period, Saul turned like a leaf when David started to become more popular among the people. Finally, David even had to flee for his life. The tough years in which he got hunted down were finally over when King Saul died on the battlefield. After a period of seven years in which he only reigned over the tribe of Judah, he became king over the whole of Israel. The promise of God finally went into fulfillment. David had also conquered Jerusalem and made it the capital of the country. He had received and accomplished much, but still, the heart of David was not satisfied. He still had one large unfulfilled desire, and it was that the ark would be in Jerusalem. David loved the Lord more than anything or anyone. He wanted the ark, the presence of God, in the center of his life and in the center of government of the country. The glory of God was the only thing that could satisfy him.

A Dead-End Road

The longing for that glory did come with a price. No carnality can stand in the way of God's glory. God had given clear instructions about how to handle the ark. David had been careless; he had not studied the guidelines God had given for the transportation of the ark. He found them out with shock when Uzza fell dead next to the ark.

Uzza's name means "**strength**." Nothing is in the Bible by coincidence! The Holy Spirit wants to show us something here. Uzza is a representation of human strength or of our flesh. We often try to reach God in our own power or receive His glory through human strength. But the Bible is clear that human strength is not the way, "not by force nor by strength, but by my Spirit, says the Lord" (Zechariah 4:6). In our own strength, we cannot do anything substantial. God does not want to share His glory with flesh; only He deserves all the honor and glory!

They used a brand-new carriage to transport the ark, but God had instructed that the Levites should carry it. They trusted human ideas instead of acting on the Word of God.

"My people are destroyed for lack of KNOWLEDGE!"

Lack of knowledge is a pitfall when it comes to our work for the Lord. We can do things from a good desire because out of love for the Lord, we want to do anything for Him. But if we trust our own great ideas, we will miss the point completely. We cannot do the will of God or bring revival by following human strategies. From the story of David, we can learn that this never leads to success. Even with the best intentions, you can reach a dead-end, and all your efforts will only leave you frustrated.

The carriage was so slick; it was brand new, the newest model. They had done their very best to organize it all well. The men who guarded the ark did so with all their hearts. Still, their efforts fell short in God's eyes. Why? Is God so hard to please? Is He so selective? Was there any sin in Uzza's life that made God strike him so hard?

We can answer all those questions with a resounding "no." The problem was that the people were doing "what seemed right in their own eyes." They did not consult with God. They had not researched God's Word to find out how He wanted it. Sometimes, you can seem to do something good from a sincere heart to serve God, but not "every good thing" is automatically also "a God thing"!

There was nothing wrong with David's heart nor his desire to bring the presence and glory of God to the center of the whole nation. God had put that desire in his heart Himself. However, he outran the Lord in his enthusiasm and assumed his own "good ideas" would be fine instead of consulting with the Lord first. 1 Samuel 6:1-8 paints a picture of this. Paul writes to the church in Corinth that the stories of the Old Testament contain lessons for us as New Testament believers so that we can avoid making the mistakes they made. The challenge is up to us to be people of the Word and find the leading of the Holy Spirit in everything!

Fortunately, God saw the heart of David, and he got a second chance. As partakers of the Covenant of grace, we know that God also sees our hearts and does not punish us for mistakes but always forgives and gives us new chances. David is one of the people who, although he lived under the Old Covenant, had many insights that belong to the New Covenant in which we live. Despite his mistakes—and who never fails?—God always saw the heart of David. That God looks at the heart was something that David had already learned in his teenage years.

David knew better than anyone that man looks at the outside, but God looks at the heart. He had experienced that when Samuel was sent to the house of his father Jesse to anoint the successor of King Saul. While his brothers were already at the feast of sacrifice, David was still outside, tending to the sheep. Jesse made "all his sons" walk past Samuel one by one. All seven passed by, and Samuel was especially impressed by the eldest son. Maybe Eliab reminded him of his first encounter with Saul. Just like Saul, Eliab was tall and handsome to see, but the Lord, who sees the heart, said to Samuel, "No, this is not the one." The Lord also spoke about the other sons, that they were not the choice for kingship. Jesse only got David when Samuel asked him if he maybe had another son. Why was David, the youngest of all, still working while all his brothers were at the feast of offerings? The Bible does not explain any further, but it is significant. As soon as David came into the house in his work clothes, straight from the flock, God spoke to Samuel, "Stand up and anoint him, this is the one." The Lord knew David, and David knew the Lord. As young as David was, he had already developed a heart-to-heart relationship with the Lord and had experienced adventures with Him, and that is why the Lord chose him.

David, "the boy after God's heart," was gradually becoming "the man after God's heart."

David received that honorary title from the Lord Himself. That is encouraging for us: Despite the mistakes David made in his life, God knew that the heart of David went out to Him. He corrected David but had never forsaken him, and that is how the Father also interacts with us.

A person looks at the outside, but God looks at the heart. It is impossible to speak about our desire for God's glory without paying attention to the things of our hearts. It is our heart where God makes His home. Therefore, let us be more focused on internal things than external things. Let us make a decision to let the Holy Spirit do His work IN US.

If we want to be part of the glorious church, then a continuous transforming work needs to take place IN us. It is so comfortable to dance around that nice carriage, "Look guys, look how well we have organized this." God was not impressed then, and also, in our time, He is not impressed by "our good ideas." They danced and skipped for the Lord but showed that they did not really know His heart by doing things their own way, a characteristic of stubborn people. We can be busy with all kinds of spiritual activities, but do we know the Lord? Do we know His Word? Do we know His heart? He looks very differently: He rejoices when we *know* Him. You can develop all kinds of spiritual activities in your personal life or in the church, but what does the Lord say that you need to do?!

"Spiritual activity is not a replacement for obedience."

For example, if you need a financial breakthrough, it is usually of little use to only pray and fast. Of course, praying and fasting can help you to align with the Holy Spirit so you can receive revelation about the key to your breakthrough. The Word of God clearly shows that a financial breakthrough is set free by giving. Until you do what the Word says about the area where you have a need, you will not see the breakthrough. The spiritual activity of praying and fasting cannot replace the obedience of giving.

Until you do THAT which God tells you to do, you will see little fruit! It requires KNOWLEDGE from God. Knowledge from God is so much more than head knowledge; it is more about revelatory knowledge! When the Holy Spirit shows you something in the Word, and you start walking in it, you will start to reap the benefits. That is walking in knowing God! You have seen it in the Word, experienced that it is true, and tasted it by stepping out and reaping the benefits: yes, nobody can take that away from you! However, it requires a humble heart that wants to submit to the Word and the Spirit. It requires a heart of submission and brokenness; it means dying to your flesh. The flesh does not want to submit and strives out of human power to see things happen. The way of the Lord is that we see our flesh as dead and instead have a deep respect for the Word and make room for the Spirit of God.

Brought to a Standstill

> *David was **afraid of the Lord** that day; and he said, "How can the ark of the Lord come to me?"*
>
> — 2 SAMUEL 6:9

He had failed in his mission and was deeply disappointed. Sometimes, things do not go the way we expected them to. Sometimes, God does not do it the way we planned. Maybe you yourself have had a desire that was not immediately fulfilled, maybe a desire for a touch of God, for the right partner, or to be healed, and it just would not happen. It is easy to throw in the towel and become disillusioned. Many people sink so deeply into disappointment that they lose hope. They no longer believe that God is doing good things for them and choose indifference to not feel the pain. The fire they once had is extinguished, and their zeal for God is lost.

When you speak about the topic of *revival*, you can sometimes notice that about people. "Yes," they say, "for years that has been prophesied so many times over the Netherlands already, I do not believe in it anymore." I also have had moments myself in which I had the temptation to become disappointed, indifferent, or throw in the towel and play safe. The question is what we do when we have that temptation. If you let the fire of the Holy Spirit burn in your heart, you cannot stay in your disappointment. The Holy Spirit will always motivate us to keep hoping, keep believing, and get moving again.

It is so beautiful to read how honestly David poured out his heart before the Lord in the book of Psalms. In unpolished words, he often shared his raw feelings of pain and disappointment with the Lord but always woven through with words of hope and faith. Psalm 42 is a Psalm like that, in which he shares his feelings with the Lord. It is moving to see what he writes in verse 7, "Deep calls to deep at the roar of your waterfalls." In my own words, David says here, "From the depth of my spirit, I call to Your Spirit." That is how the Holy Spirit moves in the depths of your heart and puts the water back into motion.

Let the hope return in your heart today, let faith return, and let the fire of God be kindled again in your heart. Dare to believe greatly again and dare to dream like a child. Dare to take steps again as if you cannot fail because if God is for you, who can be against you!

The Road from God to the Glory

David was shocked by the death of Uzzah; he was angry at God and scared. Those feelings were so strong that he essentially gave up. He let the ark take another route to the house of Obed-edom and returned back to Jerusalem disappointed and with an unfulfilled desire. Three months passed, and in that time, Obed-edom and his whole household became hugely blessed.

> *The ark of the Lord remained in the house of Obed-Edom the Gittite three months.* **And the Lord blessed Obed-Edom and all his household.** *Now it was told King David, saying, "The Lord has blessed the house of Obed-Edom and all that belongs to him, because of the ark of God."*
>
> — 2 SAMUEL 6:11-12

God's presence in your life produces a stream of blessings and life in abundance. When David heard how Obed-edom was blessed because of God's presence in his house, his dream came back to life, and hope jumped in his heart. You can almost hear David think, "If God is doing it for him, He will do it for me!" With renewed hope, he began researching the Word to see how he could bring the ark over to Jerusalem in God's way. David knew that if he wanted the ark, he needed to follow God's instructions. He knew, "God does not have to change. No, I need to change. If I want a different result than last time, I will need to do something differently. I will have to do it in

God's way!" He brought himself in line with the Word of God, and as a result, the ark could be brought over to Jerusalem with joy. The ark was placed in a tent, and David surrounded the ark with 24/7 praise and worship. What a New Testament heart did he have!

"We will have to do things in God's way!"

> *Now the Lord is the Spirit; and* **where the Spirit of the Lord is**, *there is liberty. But we all, with unveiled face, beholding as in a mirror the glory of the Lord, are being transformed into the same image from glory to glory, just as by the Spirit of the Lord.*
>
> — 2 CORINTHIANS 3:17, 18

God's glory in your life means a life of continuous submission to the Holy Spirit. What He wants is important, not what we want. We can learn to conform to His will and guidance, as Jesus lived out before us. Jesus, the imprint of His being and the radiation of God's glory said, "I do nothing unless I see my Father do it." He lived in total submission.

Have I already arrived there? Far from it. But am I on my way? Yes, definitely. Let us take the words of John the Baptist as guidance, "He must become more and I less."

Experience with God's Glory

In the summer of 2006, I gave my life to Jesus. A few months later, two of my brothers wanted to go to a conference in London. They asked if I wanted to come, but I thought it was a bizarre idea to fly all the way to London and then sit in meetings for a whole weekend. My brothers clearly had more spiritual hunger than I had at that moment. If you are hungry for God, you want to invest all your time and money with love because you really want to be in places where your hunger is satisfied. My hunger was not as large yet, but my brothers convinced me when they said, "Dad does not mind paying for our tickets." Well, a free trip to London, how bad could it be? With that thought in mind, I happily stepped on the plane, not knowing that the course of my whole life was about to change.

Once in London, we made sure to be at the location on time for the first meeting. We arrived hours in advance, and we were not the only early birds: Crowds of people were already waiting in line to get a good seat. Once the doors opened, we had to run to find a spot somewhere in row hundred-and-something. Every night was amazing. The first night, I was on the floor laughing and crying during the whole meeting, overwhelmed by God's presence. Nobody had prayed for me; God touched me. My head did not understand, but it was wonderful, so I let it happen to me.

On the final night, during the worship, the whole atmosphere in the room changed. It was as if an ocean of God's holiness and love poured out over us.

The man of God who led the service stepped backward on the stage and did nothing for a long time: He did not speak but just stood there. Everywhere in the sanctuary, rejoicing broke loose, and people were healed, touched, and delivered. Everything seemed to happen at the same time. It was the glory of God in a tangible way, indescribably beautiful, a sneak preview of what heaven will soon be like for us. When this was all over, the man of God stepped forward again and said that this had only happened a few times in his tens of years of ministry. He had seen Jesus walk in the sanctuary and seen people healed by His touch that night. Then he said, "Because tonight is such a special night, I feel the Lord saying that whatever you ask of Him, He will give you." There I was sitting, just saved for a few months. What do I ask the Lord? What do I want more than anything? The Holy Spirit birthed something inside my heart that night. My request to the Lord was, "Give us revival in the Netherlands."

That moment has marked my life forever. I cannot get away from it. Revival is burnt into my heart. I do not know how, and I do not know what, but I do know that it is a Godly desire straight out of the heart of the Father. A Church ablaze, a Church with great impact in this world, a Church as in Acts, and a Church that shines with the glory of God!

2
THE GLORIOUS CHURCH SHINES!

> *Arise, shine; For your light has come! And the glory of the Lord is risen upon you. For behold, the darkness shall cover the earth, And deep darkness the people; But the Lord will arise over you, And His glory will be seen upon you. The Gentiles shall come to your light, And kings to the brightness of your rising.*
>
> — ISAIAH 60:1-3

Have you ever woken up in the middle of the night and walked down the stairs to the living room in the dark to turn on the light, half sleeping? In the blink of an eye, you go from complete darkness to a sea of light! You blink your eyes a few times because you first have to adjust to the bright light. We, as the Church, will shine in that way in a world that is getting darker: It will spread a sea of light to places where darkness seems to reign.

> *You are the light of the world. A city that is set on a hill **cannot be hidden!***
>
> — MATTHEW 5:14

Jesus said we are the light of the world. We often give this too little thought! With almost a false modesty, we are more aware of the fact that Jesus was the light of the world when He walked on earth. That also was the case. Everywhere He came during His walk on earth, He spread that light. However, we must understand that Jesus has not been here since His ascension; His work here on earth was done. It is now up to us, His Body here on earth, to let that light shine. The Spirit of Jesus lives in us, and He wants to shine His light in the darkest places through us.

"The Glorious Church that Jesus is raising up in these days is a Church that shines with the light of Jesus."

This Glorious Church will be shining with God's glory in such a way that it will touch the entire world. The Church will have an impact on every nation of this world! The light will shine brightly in the darkness! People will be attracted by that light. That is why Jesus firmly planted that in the hearts of the disciples, "You are the light of the world." He made it clear that it was not allowed to stay hidden; it had to be visible to everyone, as a city on the hill and as a lamp on a stand. Visible light drives out darkness. If the light remains hidden from the world, we are a church without influence.

In all honesty, the world does not notice when we have meetings together within the walls of our buildings. As believers, we come together to worship God and be empowered by the Word and the Spirit. The world will only notice if we let the light of God's glory shine through us and bring transformation. Our light has been hidden for too long. We have been too focused on activities within the walls of our buildings. Too often, the message has been focused on how we can grow and change: "The battle *you* are facing," or "Seven steps how you can overcome disappointment," etc. Such messages are also necessary, of course. But if that is the focus, we will be looking inward and at ourselves. Then the danger that we miss the goal of the Christian life completely is right around the corner because we are called to lose our own life for Him, His will, and the desires of His heart. We are supposed to give our lives for other people out of love. We are called to serve the world with our time, energy, finances, and talents. The core of the Christian life is selfless, unconditional love. That means dying to yourself and committing your life to God and His kingdom. If that is not the focus within the Body of Christ, we will slowly bleed to death.

The Bible illustrates in Ezekiel 47 the river that flows out of God's throne and into the sea. Everywhere the river flows, everything comes to life, except for the pools and swamps. Why is that? The reason is simple: because the water cannot flow through there! Water flows in, but no water flows out. What a lesson for us! The Spirit of God inside us wants to flow to a dry and thirsty world to bring the life of God there, from the throne to the sea.

On the final day of the Feast of Tabernacles, Jesus stood up and cried out with a loud voice, "If anyone thirsts, let him come to Me and drink. He who believes in Me, as the Scripture has said, out of his heart will flow rivers of living water." (John 7:37, 38).

Our thirst was quenched when the Spirit came to live in us, and we were born again, but He also wants to flow out of us to the thirsty people around us. That is why it is so crucial that we keep the great commission in mind that Jesus has given to us all. If we want to grow and flourish in our relationship with the Lord, then His heart's desire to reach every lost person on this earth with His love should also be our heart's desire. After all, He does not want even one person to be lost, but that all are saved, and He can only reach them through us, His body here on earth, the Church, you, and me.

In Proverbs, it is stated that "the generous soul will be made rich, and he who waters will also be watered himself" (Proverbs 11:25). You could describe it in this way: "the one who pours out his life to bless others will themselves be satisfied."

2 Kings 4 tells the story of a poor widow who illustrates this principle beautifully. She was the woman of one of the prophets who functioned in the ministry of the prophet Elisha, but unfortunately, her husband had died. While she was mourning the loss of her husband, she also had to deal with an enormous problem. Because of a debt she and her husband had, and that they under no circumstance could pay, the lender threatened to take her two sons away from her as slaves. This poor woman was about to lose everything precious to her. Fortunately, she is sensible enough to come to Elisha with her problem. To her surprise, he asks her a counter question, "What do you have in your house?" What a nonsensical question! She just came to Elisha because she has nothing! If she had anything, then she would not have had to call the prophet for help. She had already thought of everything and sought every possible solution, but she had not been able to think of anything; she was desperate: "After all, she had nothing." But the prophet was waiting for a reply to his question, so she tells him how awful her situation is, "I have nothing in my house, except for a jar of oil." A jar of oil is "something," but in her eyes, it was "nothing." The prophet knew better! He knew that if we give our "something," even

if it is "nothing" in our eyes, into the hands of God, it will turn out to be more than enough. With God, a little becomes a whole lot if we simply use it.

Elisha gave her the assignment to gather as many jars, in every shape and form—that did not matter—as long as it was a vessel. She did her best and asked all her neighbors, family members, and acquaintances for jars. She does not care if they find it a crazy demand; the prophet said so, and she trusts his word. Finally, her whole house is full of vessels. She closes the doors and starts pouring her little jar of oil into the vessels. Then the miracle happens: The little bit of oil multiplies while it is being poured. All the vessels are being filled; the oil keeps on flowing! Only when the final vessel is full, and no empty vessels are left, does the oil stop flowing.

> **"With God, a little becomes a whole lot if we simply use it."**

What an illustration for us as believers today! The Bible teaches us that we all have a treasure in our earthly vessels. Our body is that vessel, and the Spirit is the treasure. We are like that little jar of oil. We look at ourselves and maybe think, "It is nothing": our talents seem so minimal, our boldness so substandard, and our anointing not impressive; what good can come out of that? What is "nothing" in our eyes is "something" in the eyes of the Lord, which He can use to let a stream of blessing come forth out of. But that is only possible if we simply start pouring! We do not have to worry about the "but how." Our responsibility is to be obedient in childlike simplicity. The mission Jesus gave to the

Church seems overwhelming, and sometimes, we ask ourselves how we could ever accomplish it. Start pouring, says the Lord. Start pouring the oil you carry in you, and start pouring it into the empty vessels around you. As long as there are empty vessels, the oil will keep flowing. There are loads of empty vessels all around us. Let us take our eyes off of ourselves, not looking at how small our little jar is, but have our eyes focused on God and start to pour in faith. If we do that, we will have an enormous impact on this generation in our time. If we do that, we will see miracles!

The Great Commission

Before Jesus went to heaven, He gave His disciples His last instructions. Someone's last words are always important, especially if they are the last words of the reigning King.

> *But you shall receive power when the Holy Spirit has come upon you; and you shall be witnesses to Me in Jerusalem, and in all Judea and Samaria, and to the end of the earth.*
>
> — ACTS 1:8

Immediately after He said this, He ascended, and while they saw that happen, a cloud took Him away from their eyes. It was expected of the disciples who stayed behind that they would take the instructions of Jesus to heart. They would receive power. For what? To get goosebumps? To organize nice meetings and conferences? No, no, no. They would receive the power to be His witnesses! To start with, in their own city, then in their region and country, and from there, to all the other countries of the world. The mission was clear!

> *And He said to them, "Go into all the world and*
> *preach the gospel to every creature.*
>
> — MARK 16:15

Go! Get out there! Go into all the world. Tell the good news. Be My witnesses!

The degree of life in a congregation can be measured by the emphasis on reaching lost souls. If there is no emphasis on that, the chance is high that there is little life there. Why is that? Because the Holy Spirit—The Spirit of LIFE—has come to give us the power to be witnesses. To be frank, it is the primary function of the Holy Spirit to witness of Jesus! He can only do that through us. So, if we do not witness, the Holy Spirit cannot fulfill His task on earth. The Holy Spirit looks for people who witness and for churches where that is a high priority. He will be more expressly present in places where His primary function is taken seriously. Logical, right?

As the pastor of a local church, I can witness how great it is to be part of a church full of soulwinners. Every week, teams go on the streets and into the neighborhoods to share Jesus with the people of our city. Next to this, there is essentially no Sunday that passes without someone responding to the altar call. Weekly, people are being won for Jesus! In our own country! This is not just for *the mission field* or evangelical campaigns in other parts of the world. This is for here, and this is for now! Europe is a gigantic mission field, and God is holding us accountable for our generation. If we do not reach them, who will? If we do not tell them, who will? We can pray for revival until we cannot anymore, but revival starts in us.

Revival starts IN the believer. The disciples in the upper room became full of the Holy Spirit, they received power, and then, they went outside immediately, where a crowd of people had gathered to witness of Jesus. Let us let the river of the Holy Spirit flow through us to a generation that thirsts for the living water!

Covered

It is God's desire to see the whole earth covered with His glory. When He created Adam and Eve, He gave them the command to fill the earth and to make it submit. They were clothed with His glory and had delegated authority to rule on this earth. Unfortunately, they failed by giving an ear to the lies of Lucifer. They gave their place of authority to him and were no longer "glory-carriers" but naked. God the Son came as a human to restore everything. He settled the sin problem on the cross so that whoever believes in Him has the recovery of honor. Before His ascension to heaven, Jesus shared with His disciples that He now had all authority in heaven and on earth. That authority He has delegated to the Church, the mission is resumed, and every born-again believer is a *glory-carrier* and can participate to see God's desire become fulfilled.

> *For the earth will be filled with the knowledge of the glory of the Lord, as the waters* **cover** *the sea.*
>
> — HABAKKUK 2:14

What does that mean practically? It sounds so beautiful, but how can we participate in that? The Lord has also given us an answer to that. We have received the command to go into all the world and preach the gospel to the whole of creation, to make all peoples His disciples. In that way, we can participate in filling the earth with "the knowledge of the glory of the Lord." Again, that is not about "intellectual knowledge." It is about "knowing Jesus Christ intimately" and "knowing who He is in all His glory." If each person on earth would *know* Him, the earth would be covered with the knowledge of His glory.

Jesus is the Image of the Invisible God. The disciple John witnessed of Him, "And the Word became flesh and dwelt among us, and we beheld His glory, the glory as of the only begotten of the Father, full of grace and truth" (John 1:14). Peter, James, and John had the enormous privilege to be taken on a high mountain by Jesus, where He changed appearance in front of their eyes. His face shined like the sun, and His clothes became white as light. John was an eyewitness of the glory of Jesus, and he was allowed to glance at who Jesus truly was. He is God become human, God the Son that walked on this earth incognito and gave His life to save us. The disciples also had trouble truly understanding who He was. Jesus tried to make it clear for Philip, who had been spending time with Him for years already, "He who has seen Me has seen the Father" (John 14:9). In these times, many people also do not see Him because their mind is blinded by the devil. God wants every human to get to know Him, but the devil does everything in his power so they do not get to know Him.

> *But even if our gospel is veiled, it is veiled to those who are perishing, whose minds the god of this age has blinded, who do not believe, lest the light of the gospel of the glory of Christ, who is the image of God, should shine on them.*
>
> —2 CORINTHIANS 4:3, 4

The devil has blindfolded people, so to speak, so that they cannot see the light. The only remedy is prayer and preaching. We can pray for people that their eyes are opened for Jesus, but it is the preaching of the Word that can bypass their minds and reach their hearts. That is the power of the Gospel! The Gospel does not so much speak to the mind of the human but to their heart. The mind can wrestle with what is being spoken, while the heart opens to receive from the Lord. It is the foolishness of preaching, but God has decided in His wisdom to offer salvation to the lost in that way (1 Corinthians 1:18-25, Romans 1:1-16).

"If you know Him, you want to make Him known."

How can the earth become full of the KNOWLEDGE of God's GLORY if His children have no KNOWLEDGE of His GLORY? This knowledge is not head-knowledge. It is revelatory knowledge, heart-knowledge, and experience-knowledge. If you know Him, you want to make Him known!

A Church with Influence

The Church in the last days will be a Church of great influence.

> *Now it shall come to pass in the latter days that the mountain of the Lord's house shall be established on the top of the mountains, and shall be exalted above the hills;*
> *And all nations shall flow to it. Many people shall come and say, "Come, and let us go up to the mountain of the Lord, to the house of*

> *the God of Jacob; He will teach us His ways,
> and we shall walk in His paths."*
>
> —ISAIAH 2:2, 3

John G. Lake worked as a missionary from 1908 until 1913 in South Africa. In his book *Adventures in God,* he tells the story of Dan van Vuuren.

Dan van Vuuren was a butcher in South Africa until he got tuberculosis and had to sell his business because of his illness. He moved to a farm in the countryside, hoping that after his death, his wife would be able to live off the proceeds. At that time, he received a letter from Johannesburg from someone who was miraculously healed. In that letter, he read about how his niece was filled with the Holy Spirit and many other miraculous things God had done in that region.

Dan took the letter, knelt under an African thornbush, and cried out to God. The hunger in him took over everything else. As the Bible says: "deep calls out to deep" and "blessed are they that hunger, because they WILL be filled." While he was kneeling and crying out there, a great miracle happened because, within ten minutes, he was fully healed.

Dan had been praying for the salvation of his wife for ten years, but now, after one look at him, she gave her heart to Jesus. Within a week, all of his eleven children were saved and filled with the Holy Spirit, and after a couple of weeks, nineteen other families were saved and filled with the Holy Spirit.

God spoke the following to Dan, "Go to all the members of parliament and tell them about Me."

The Lord opened the door for a visit to Louis Botha, the president at that time.

This is what Botha himself said about this meeting in retrospect:

> *I knew Van Vuuren from our youth. I knew him as a reckless man. But that man came into my office that day and stood three meters away from my desk. I looked up, and before he could speak a word, I started shaking in my chair. I knelt, put my head under the desk, and cried out to God. He looked like God, he spoke like God, he had the majesty of God. It was supernaturally miraculous.*

For eighteen days, Dan visited the different offices of the members of parliament. He also visited the lawyers, judges, and other highly placed members of the country until they all knew there was a God. They all heard about Christ the Savior and the baptism in the Holy Spirit, and all because Dan van Vuuren had hungered for God. He had hungered for God, got clothed with the glory of God, and had a great impact for God. Let us cry out to God just like Dan van Vuuren until we are so full of Him that everyone we come in contact with sees Jesus in our eyes and Jesus in our voice.

God desires that we desire Him. There have always been people with that hunger in their hearts, and you can say about every one of them that they have made a great impact on their generation and even the generations after them.

In the Old Testament, we read about Moses. He had a burning desire to know God face to face. He had already experienced so much with God, heard His voice so often, and seen so many miracles, but the desire to know God intimately had only grown. The cry of his heart was, "Show me Your glory."

David also was consumed by a desire to know God intimately and to be in His presence. That is why he brought the ark to Jerusalem. We can read the cry for knowing God in the Psalms he wrote, "As the deer pants for the water brooks, so pants my soul for You, O God" (Psalm 42:1).

Paul had a similar experience. He was a wholehearted persecutor of Christians. Because of his religious beliefs, he was full of anger toward the supporters of "that Jesus," and he worked rigorously to take them captive and bring them to trial. On his way to Damascus to also persecute the Christians there, a bright light suddenly shined around him. He fell on the ground and was blind for three days. While that light shined around him, he heard the voice of Jesus, who called him for the ministry. Paul was transformed at once from persecutor to builder of the Church. One encounter with Jesus, and you will never be the same! Before, he could see, but he was spiritually blind. After his meeting with Jesus, he was blind for three days, but his spiritual eyes opened. He had literally *"seen the Light"*. Only Jesus can do that, and He still wants to meet people today. That does not always happen in such a dramatic way like with Paul, but maybe just through you and me. If you have had an encounter with Jesus, then that is visible on your face. If you know that He lives and that He lives IN YOU, then that will be visible to the people around you.

Jesus wants to have a meeting with you, an encounter that transforms your life. Many have theology without an experience, but that is not worth much. Christianity is an experience. You need to experience it! You can read about someone in a book, but getting to know someone personally is a completely different experience. That is what God wants with you and me. Jesus said, "And THIS is eternal life, that they may *know* You, the only true God, and Jesus Christ whom You have sent" (John 17:3). You have not received eternal life by becoming a member of a church or because you have grown up in a Christian family. You have received it because you have gotten to know Jesus yourself. You have gotten to know God the Father as your Father! If you know Him, you can make Him known to the world around you. That was what Paul lived for after his encounter with Jesus:

> *Yes, everything else is worthless when compared with the infinite value of knowing Christ Jesus my Lord. For his sake I have discarded everything else, counting it all as garbage, so that I could gain Christ and become one with him. I no longer count on my own righteousness through obeying the law; rather, I become righteous through faith in Christ. For God's way of making us right with himself depends on faith. I want to know Christ and experience the mighty power that raised him from the dead. I want to suffer with him, sharing in his death, so that one way or another I will experience the resurrection from the dead!*
>
> — PHILIPPIANS 3:8-11 NLT

Paul says: I have gotten to know Jesus, and compared to Him, everything from my old life is nothing more than garbage. He is so amazingly beautiful, so good, so powerful, and wonderful; everything else fades compared to Him, but I want more. I will not settle with only the first encounter—however great that was—but I am hungry for more. I am reaching out for more of Jesus. I want to get to know Him even better.

I want to walk in His light. I want to see His face. That persistent hunger came forth out of Paul's first encounter with Jesus on the road to Damascus. And he often witnessed of it, among other things. After his arrest in Jerusalem, he talked about it to King Agrippa.

> *I journeyed to Damascus ... at midday, O king, along the road I saw a light from heaven, brighter than the sun, shining around me and those who journeyed with me.*
>
> — ACTS 26:12, 13

Paul saw a great light, stronger than the shining of the sun. He saw Jesus in His glory, and out of that light, Jesus started to speak to him, and He gave him the calling for his life.

> "But rise and stand on your feet; for I have appeared to you for this purpose, to make you a minister and a witness both of the things which you have seen and of the things which I will yet reveal to you. I will deliver you from the Jewish people, as well as from the Gentiles, to whom I now send you, to open their eyes, in order to turn them from darkness to light, and from the power of Satan to God, that they may receive forgiveness of sins and an inheritance among those who are sanctified by faith in Me."
>
> — ACTS 26:16-18

His whole life was transformed at once. Suddenly, he had a God-given mission to convert people from the darkness to that light. That radiating light had an enormous impact on Paul, and it was an experience he would never forget. Everywhere he went, he testified of that Light of Jesus Christ. Kings, emperors, statesmen, prominent people, and esteemed people all got to hear the gospel. God's mission has not changed today. The Great Commission is not the great suggestion. It is the command of Jesus, and we should take it seriously. I have noticed in my own life that if I pour out what I have and let the river flow to others, I myself get blessed. To say it less cryptically: If I reach others with the gospel of Jesus Christ, I get encouraged and refreshed myself. It is precisely in the stepping out in obedience that the blessing is.

As the church, our whole right of existence is also that we are saved to save others. Many want a ministry, but how many are already stepping out in the ministry of all believers: the ministry of reconciliation? (2 Cor. 5:18). There is a ripe harvest outside of the four church walls, and it is both our privilege and responsibility to tell that the door of grace is wide open.

> *For "whoever calls on the name of the Lord shall be saved." How then shall they call on Him in whom they have not believed? And how shall they believe in Him of whom they have not heard? And how shall they hear without a preacher?*
>
> — ROMANS 10:13, 14

How will they believe in Jesus if nobody tells them about Jesus? In our evangelization work in the Netherlands, we often marvel at how many people have no concept of who Jesus is. A whole generation of young people has never been in a church, has not been raised with the Bible, and knows next to nothing about Jesus. That is our mission field! The fields are white to harvest in the Netherlands, but there are not enough laborers. I believe the Holy Spirit is still working to raise up laborers in the Church who want to put their hands to the plow and help bring in the harvest. The beautiful thing is that everyone can do their part.

In the River Amsterdam, we have set a goal to raise a Gideon-like army of three hundred laborers in the harvest. We will split this army of three hundred into three groups like Gideon did with his army. We stand in faith to raise up a hundred full-time evangelists for Europe, a hundred leaders with a pastoral heart who can care for the new disciples, and a hundred multi-millionaires who can finance the work. We are continuously active with this within the congregation and our Bible school. Time is short. Jesus is coming back soon; now is the time to make your life count for eternity! Everybody can do something. You only need to find your area and remain faithful; then God will entrust you more and more, and you will be a crucial part of bringing in this end-time harvest.

He is raising up a glorious Church, shining with the light of the Gospel, especially in the darkest places. What a privilege to be part of that end-time Church and to have an impact on this generation in these times!

3

THE GLORIOUS CHURCH RADIATES

That He might present her to Himself a glorious church, not having spot or wrinkle or any such thing, but that she should be holy and without blemish.

— EPHESIANS 5:27

God is building a Glorious Church.

A Church full of His glory.

A Church so full of His glory that every person who comes into contact with it is transformed.

A Church that has influence in the city.

A Church so full of the Holy Spirit that signs and wonders are the standard of the day.

A Church so full of God's glory that the world gets changed by it.

A Church that has the answer to the needs of the people.

A Body of people so hungry for God, and God alone, that everything else fades. We are that Body!

A church without spots or wrinkles or anything similar…

Is that possible? A church of which the people live pure and holy and who radiate God's glory? Yes, that is a hundred percent possible. Otherwise, the Holy Spirit would not have described it like that in Ephesians 5. Can this be cultivated by people? No, this is the work of the Word and the Spirit. Can we participate in that plan? Yes, definitely! Jesus gave the fivefold ministry to the church to make her mature and to equip her for the work of service. If we receive the messengers of God in that way, we can already make great leaps. More on that in the chapter about unity.

Holy and Spotless

In these times in the preaching, the emphasis is not put on holiness as much. Yet, that is still an enormously important work the Holy Spirit wants to do in every believer. God strongly desires a holy church that is set apart for Him. He does everything in His power to start this sanctification process in every believer.

In my experience as a pastor, I have noticed that there are two essential things necessary to see progress in the process of sanctification.

Firstly, the place of the Word in the believer's life is essential. In Ephesians 5, Paul speaks of the marriage relationship between husband and wife in the context of how Jesus, as Bridegroom, deals with His Bride. He makes it clear that He sanctifies His Bride by cleansing her with the Word.

> *That He might sanctify and cleanse her with the washing of water by the word.*
>
> — EPHESIANS 5:26

The Word of God is alive and powerful; His Words are spirit and life. **When you read the Word, it reads you.** It corrects you, gives you instructions for your life, is a mirror held in front of you, and encourages and strengthens you. What bread is to your body, the Word is to your spirit.

"When you read the Word, it reads you."

> *'Man shall not live by bread alone, but by every word that proceeds from the mouth of God.'*
>
> — MATTHEW 4:4

As a preacher of the Word, I make sure that I do not get carried away by the spirit of this time and drift away from the preaching of the living Word of God. Jesus has called pastors and preachers to bring the Word, not to give talks as if we are psychologists or life coaches. He has commanded us to preach the gospel to the whole of creation. The Word is what makes the difference.

Jesus told the parable of the sower and explained it to His disciples as the basis for all other parables. Jesus said that if you do not understand this parable, you will not understand all the other parables either. What is the essence of that parable? Firstly, Jesus made it clear that the Word needs to be sowed into the fields of the hearts of people. He also emphasized that the Word produces fruit in the lives of those who receive the Word with faith and hold onto it with perseverance in their hearts. **Less Word is less seed and automatically leads to less fruit in people's lives. More Word is more seed and leads to a greater harvest of fruit.** The people who grow the fastest are the people who take the Word seriously. If we want to see a glorious Church arise in our country, we will need to preach the Word with renewed dedication because the Word of God in the hearts of the listeners will eventually lead to fruit in their lives.

As an individual believer, you, of course, are primarily responsible for filling yourself with the Word of God. Most people eat three meals a day to feed their bodies but give their spirits one light snack a week. The fact of the matter is we do not have enough with that one meal a week that is served to us in the church. With such a spiritual diet, you're not going to grow! Such a diet will lead to spiritual anorexia, and instead of spiritual growth, spiritual life gets even weaker; the flesh gets the upper hand with all its consequences. It might sound pessimistic, but fortunately, I am not. To my great joy, I see that many Christians in these times have a renewed hunger for the Word of God. They are people who do not settle for ear-pleasing messages that are nice to the soul but people who crave truth. They realize how true it is what Jesus said: "If you abide in my word, you are truly my disciples, and you will know the truth, and the truth shall make you free" (John 8:31-32). The Word produces fruit and blessings in our lives.

> *Blessed is the man who walks not in the counsel of the ungodly, nor stands in the path of sinners, nor sits in the seat of the scornful; but his delight is in the law of the Lord, and in His law he meditates day and night. He*

> *shall be like a tree planted by the rivers of water, that brings forth its fruit in its season, whose leaf also shall not wither; and whatever he does shall prosper.*
>
> — PSALM 1:1-3

You obtain a clean and holy life by diving in and getting washed often by the water of the Word. When you do that, your mind gets renewed. The Word does not just rinse away your desire to sin. It does so much more! The Word of God is more than letters on paper; it is alive and powerful! Every time you open your Bible and read His words, you sow the life of God into your insides. You are infused with heavenly truth and the DNA of God. An inner transformation takes place by the imperishable seed of the Word. A godly life is not a life of "nothing-is-allowed-and-everything-must-be-done." It is a life overflowing with blessing, peace, and joy.

Think about Adam before the fall. Did Adam have a boring life? No. On the contrary, he lived as a king in this world in a place of mega abundance, enjoying God's good gifts. When sin crept into the hearts of man, and they rebelled against God, it took with it all the misery we are familiar with. Sin is a robber, but God is the Rewarder.

If we, as sons and daughters of God, want to reflect His glory in this world, then that is impossible without the Word. Jesus is the Word made flesh, and He said that if we remain in Him, we will carry much fruit. That fruit does not come from our smart ideas or hard work. It comes forth out of the Word that produces in us what God has sent it for. It produces healing, prosperity, blessing, and life in abundance. It produces freedom, sonship, and yoke-breaking power by revelation. It also produces the character of God in us.

The Word causes us to become reflections of the Son of God!

> **"There is nothing wrong with you that a revelation out of the Word cannot fix."**

A pastor once said to me, "If someone in my congregation comes to me for counseling, I give them this advice: First, come to all meetings for a month, every Sunday morning, Sunday evening, and Wednesday evening. If you still need counseling after that month, we can talk." He said that nine out of ten people do not need counseling anymore after that month. The Word had done the work.

I myself regularly experience that someone comes up to me after the meeting and tells me that the message was exactly what he or she needed to hear. The Lord knows what people are going through and gives everyone what he or she needs. Some church members ask jokingly if I have hung cameras in their houses to know what they are doing and saying so I can talk about it on Sunday. Obviously, I have no clue what they are doing, and to be honest, I also do not want to know. But the Holy Spirit knows everything! As Jesus broke the bread and gave the crowd food to eat, the Holy Spirit breaks the Word of God when we preach it and feeds the crowd with it. One message can be heard by hundreds of people, and each one of them can take something from it very personally for themselves. That is only possible because the Word is living and supernatural!

Secondly, the work of the Holy Spirit is essential to be holy and spotless as the Bride of Christ for His coming. It is so important that we have the right balance and do not get carried away to one side at the expense of the other side: only the Word and too little room for the Spirit, or only the Spirit and too little accent on the Word. It is an old saying but still relevant today: "With only the Word, you dry up; only the Spirit, you blow up; but through the Word and Spirit together, you grow up." The Word and the Spirit are inseparably connected, and we desperately need both. The Holy Spirit is there for so much more than to give us a euphoric feeling or to make us cry during a meeting. He came to change us into the image of Jesus! If He gets too little space in our meetings to do His work in people, there will also be limited growth and fruit in people's lives. As leaders, we need to know our place. He is the Lord, and we are His servants, not the other way around! The Holy Spirit decides what a meeting is allowed to look like, so it is important that we give Him the space and are sensitive to His leading.

The same principle goes for our individual lives as believers. He gets to decide the course. He leads, and we follow. Too often, the tender personality of the Holy Spirit is treated with too little respect, and He remains waiting like a gentleman until there is space made for Him so that He can do what He wants. Praise Him for the abundance of His grace, that He is patient with us and keeps giving us new chances to learn and to grow!

The Holy Spirit does not only work the process of sanctification in us through the water of the Word but also through the fire! He is the Baptizer with fire, and the fire of the Holy Spirit wants to do a cleansing work in us.

Fire Makes You Pure

> *John answered, saying to all, "I indeed baptize*
> *you with water; but One mightier than I is*
> *coming, whose sandal strap I am not worthy*

> to loose. He will baptize you with the Holy
> Spirit and fire.
>
> — LUKE 3:16

Most born-again Christians are familiar with the importance of baptism with (or in) the Holy Spirit and have experienced it themselves. But what does *"and fire"* mean? How do you picture that? On the day of Pentecost, the believers in the upper room were baptized with the Holy Spirit and fire. The fire was even visible as tongues of fire that spread on each of them. God has not changed. He wants to set every believer on fire! That fire does not only give you a passion for the things of God, but it is also a cleansing fire.

> *But who can endure the day of His coming? And*
> *who can stand when He appears? For He is*
> *like a refiner's fire and like launderers' soap.*
> *He will sit as a refiner and a purifier of silver;*
> *He will purify the sons of Levi, and purge them*
> *as gold and silver, that they may offer to the*
> *Lord an offering in righteousness.*
>
> — MALACHI 3:2-3

Jesus came as a refiner to cleanse His people. A refiner takes the silver or gold that still has all kinds of impurities in it that take its shine and holds it in and over the fire. The fire causes the precious metal to melt, which causes the present impure components to come up. When the refiner sees that happen, he takes a kind of scoop with which he scoops away the impure upper layer. This process happens a couple of times until the refiner can see his own reflection in the molten silver or gold. If he sees his own face in the reflection, he knows it has been purified. The Lord wants to do the exact same with us by burning the fire of the Holy Spirit in us. It is a cleansing fire that brings up the impurities of our hearts. For us, that process is uncomfortable and confronting. But it is better to embrace it because it is essential for our growth toward a mature son or daughter of God. That fire burns every impurity away layer by layer until the Lord can see more and more of His own reflection in us.

Fire Now or Fire Later

> *For no other foundation can anyone lay than that which is laid, which is Jesus Christ. Now if anyone builds on this foundation with gold, silver, precious stones, wood, hay, straw, each one's work will become clear; for the Day will declare it, because it will be revealed by fire; and the fire will test each one's work, of what sort it is. If anyone's work which he has built on it endures, he will receive a reward. If anyone's work is burned, he will suffer loss; but he himself will be saved, yet so as through fire.*
>
> —1 CORINTHIANS 3:11-15

The fire will do its work anyway. We can choose if we let ourselves be cleansed by that fire or rather withdraw from it. One day, however, we will stand before the throne of grace of Christ, and our life's work will be laid on the altar to be tested by the fire of God. Then, it will be made public if it can stand the test of fire. Firstly, it is important to note that it is the throne of grace where we are held accountable for our lives, not the throne of judgment. If you are in Christ, you are saved for eternity. So, this is not about *where* you will spend eternity, heaven or hell, but this is about *how* you will spend eternity: with or without rewards.

The Holy Spirit shows us two types of materials with which we can build: flammable or inflammable materials—wood, hay, and straw, or gold, silver, and precious stones. The first category burns when it comes into contact with fire; the second category does not burn but gets even more pure when it comes into contact with fire. On that day, there will be people who have lived their entire Christian life for themselves, and everything they have done on earth will have no value for eternity. Others who have given their earthly life for heavenly, eternal purposes will stand there. As Jesus taught us in Matthew 6, they have lived to receive heavenly treasures "where neither moth nor rust destroys and where thieves do not break in and steal." The believers who have done that will receive eternal rewards and go into heaven with treasures. What a wonderful prospect that is! They will not stand before Jesus empty-handed but will lay their treasures at His feet to worship Him! What an honor!

The best choice is, of course, to let the fire do its work *now* and to ask the Lord to burn everything away that is not of Him so that He can cleanse us. If we let Him into the deepest of our being, He will even uncover and cleanse the hidden motivations and contemplations of our hearts so that we are not only pure and clean in our actions but also in our motives, thoughts, and desires. Especially those deep things can only be transformed by the fire of the Holy Spirit. If we let Him do His work, He will burn God's desires and motivations into our hearts so that we no longer live for our own interests but truly become people who act out of selfless love. Jesus was motivated by that love; He was moved by compassion. Let us not miss our goal by trying to do all kinds of things for God from personal ambition or to prove ourselves. Let the Lord burn in our hearts so that our motives, thoughts, feelings, words, and deeds are purified, and we become that clean Bride He is coming back for. Then, we will stand before Him with treasures with which we can worship Him in eternity.

A Church Full of the Holy Spirit!

> *And being assembled together with them, He commanded them not to depart from Jerusalem, but to wait for the Promise of the Father, "which," He said, "you have heard from Me; for John truly baptized with water, but you shall be baptized with the Holy Spirit not many days from now." But you shall receive power when the Holy Spirit has come upon you; and you shall be witnesses to Me in Jerusalem, and in all Judea and Samaria, and to the end of the earth."*
>
> — ACTS 1:4-5, 8

Jesus wants to BAPTIZE you with the Holy Spirit. He does not only want to fill you, He wants you to be so full that you overflow. As a cup submerged in a bathtub STAYS submerged so that you cannot separate the water from the cup, that is how full He wants us! This is the only way to live the real Christian life. **Christian is *Christ-Like*, and He had the Spirit without measure. How could we think that we can do it in our own strength?** No, let us surrender ourselves, become empty of ourselves, to be filled with God's Spirit. Let Him take the upper hand and sit on the throne of your heart.

In the Old Testament, the physical temple was filled with the glory of God. In the New Testament, the spiritual temple is filled with the glory of God. That temple is the Body of Christ. That is us individually but also corporately. God's desire is for a Body that is filled with Him. Not a few individuals that carry the glory of God, but a whole army! When that glory is seen on us, nations shall come to our light and kings to the brightness of our rising. That is God's plan for the Church. A Church that reflects Him in this world. A Church of mature sons and daughters who are His image carriers: who show Jesus everywhere they go. His Body through which He can multiply the works of Jesus on earth for every individual believer. A holy people of Spirit-filled, glorious sons and daughters, who are so full of Him that it fills the earth with the glory of the Lord. What a plan! What a privilege to be part of that plan! But also, what a responsibility to be able to work with that plan. It asks us to humbly put our plans aside and step into His plan so that He can fulfill His purposes through us.

When my wife Jacky and I still lived in America, the Lord started to speak to us about the call of God for the Netherlands. We set time apart to search Him because we wanted to clearly hear His voice. While we were praying about it, the Lord spoke the following very clearly into my heart:

"As the Netherlands has been good in keeping out water in the natural, through dams and dikes and structures of humans, so the spiritual Netherlands has also been 'good' in keeping out the water of the Holy Spirit: through religion, tradition, and structures of humans. But the dams and dikes will break, and this land will be flooded with the knowledge of the glory of the Lord."

This word exploded in me. When we walked into the office of our pastor to share with him that we experienced the call of God for the Netherlands, he pointed at me, and before I could say anything, he repeated this exact same word to me. God had clearly confirmed! Based on this word, we sold nearly all our things, handed over our positions in the ministry there, and emigrated to the Netherlands.

Many speak about how they experience spiritual drought in the Netherlands and how hard it is to be in the ministry in this country. Often, it was looked outside our borders for spiritual leaders abroad, and they were invited to bring something here in God's name. God wants to do something special here in these times, within the borders of our country, within our churches, in His Body here in the Netherlands. For that, a great awakening is needed. I believe this has already been put into motion. God does not sit still. He is raising an army of men and women, boys and girls, who want to go a hundred percent for God and are full of the Holy Spirit. An army of believers who have shown their character in the fruit of the Spirit and, at the same time, walk in the power and the gifts of the Spirit. They are people who do not flow with the normal course of action in the world but are a countermovement from the Kingdom of God. The enemy does everything to stop this, but what God has in store is not to be stopped. He is building His Church, and the gates of hell will not overwhelm her!

The Promise Fulfilled!

> *On the day of Pentecost all the believers were meeting together in one place. Suddenly, there was a sound from heaven like the roaring of a mighty windstorm, and it filled the house where they were sitting. Then,*

> *what looked like flames or tongues of fire appeared and settled on each of them. And everyone present was filled with the Holy Spirit and began speaking in other languages, as the Holy Spirit gave them this ability. At that time there were devout Jews from every nation living in Jerusalem. When they heard the loud noise, everyone came running, and they were bewildered to hear their own languages being spoken by the believers. They were completely amazed. "How can this be?" they exclaimed. "These people are all from Galilee, and yet we hear them speaking in our own native languages!" They stood there amazed and perplexed. "What can this mean?" they asked each other. But others in the crowd ridiculed them, saying, "They're just drunk, that's all!"*
>
> — ACTS 2:1-8, 12, 13 NLT

Notice that *each of them* was filled; all the believers who were together in the upper room, not just the apostles. The Holy Spirit has not come for a handful of super-apostles. He is there for *each* Christian. This gift is for everyone!

> *Peter replied, "Each of you must repent of your sins and turn to God, and be baptized in the name of Jesus Christ for the forgiveness of your sins.* **Then you will receive the gift of the Holy Spirit.** *This promise is to you, to*

> *your children, and to those far away—all*
> *who have been called by the Lord our God."*
>
> —ACTS 2:38, 39 NLT

Peter did not say that you might receive the gift of the Holy Spirit if you are righteous enough. No, he did not say that! No other conditions are set other than repentance and water baptism. Every believer is a candidate for this precious gift!

In Acts 2, we see the first church filled with the glory of God, as God had promised in Haggai. He promised, after all, that the glory of the latter house would be greater than that of the first. The temple that was rebuilt in the days of the prophet Haggai was a natural building. The future temple about which he prophesied is a spiritual building, the Body of Christ. The glory resting on the Body of Christ would far exceed the glory of the temple of Solomon. What riches the Lord has in store for His Church. On the day of Pentecost, heaven broke open, and the Holy Spirit came storming in to fill the small group of believers. The glory of God came over the first church. The people of Jerusalem heard the deafening sound of the storming wind and came to the house where the sound seemed to concentrate itself. One thing is sure: If God moves, it is visible and audible. There is no silent revival! They saw with their own eyes how a group of people flowed out and heard them speak in all kinds of languages. They were completely stunned by what they saw and heard and did not really know what to do with it. Some mockers aired their opinion loudly, "These people have had too much wine; they are so drunk! They are beside themselves! They must be drunk because this is not how a normal person behaves." That was their conclusion, and they were not too far off, actually. However, we know that they were not drunk with wine but with the Holy Spirit.

And do not be drunk with wine, in which is dissipation; but be filled with the Spirit,

— EPHESIANS 5:18

"If God moves, it is visible and audible; there is no silent revival."

Drunk with alcohol or drunk with the Spirit is a large difference: the first option is not a good idea, but becoming so full of the Holy Spirit that you seem drunk was apparently "God's idea of a good idea." Peter raised his voice above all the murmuring and started to preach, "These people are not drunk as you suppose, but this is the fulfillment of the promise that is stated in the book of Joel that God would pour His Spirit out on all flesh, on old and young, men and women." **God was preparing a Body for Himself that would be full of Him.** We do not have to settle for less than what we read in Acts 2. We might be the generation that experiences that Jesus comes for His Bride. He has kept the best wine for last, and we can freely drink from it, not a little sip, but until we are completely full as the disciples were on the day of Pentecost.

A Reflection of His Glory

In the book Song of Solomon, the Holy Spirit describes the beauty of the Bride as the beauty of the full moon, "Who is this who looks down like the dawn, beautiful as the moon, bright as the sun, awesome as an army with banners?" The moon itself does not give light, but it reflects the sun's light. The same goes for us. Our light is simply a reflection of His light that shines in us. When we let God do His work in us, through His Word and through His Spirit, that will transform us from glory to glory. We will increasingly reflect more of His glory.

When Moses was on the mountain and spent a long time in God's glory, he came off the mountain with a face that literally radiated. He had to cover his face with a veil because the glory on his face would slowly fade. Jesus also went up a mountain and was transformed before the eyes of His disciples. His face shined like the sun, and His clothes became white as light. In both situations, the glory of God became visible on a human. The Bible uses those illustrations to explain what happens to us when we allow the Spirit to transform us from within.

> *But we all, with unveiled face, beholding as in a mirror the glory of the Lord, are being transformed into the same image from glory to glory, just as by the Spirit of the Lord.*
>
> — 2 CORINTHIANS 3:18

We are constantly being transformed by the work of God's Spirit in us. Being transformed is a translation of the Greek word *metamorphoo*. In our language, we also use the word *metamorphosis*, which has the same meaning: a transformation or appearance change. The same word that is used here in Corinthians for our transformation is also used in Matthew 17:2 for the transformation of Jesus on the mountain, "And he was transfigured before them." What happened was that Jesus started to radiate like the sun before the eyes of His disciples. The glory He had in heaven before he laid everything down to come to this earth became visible. It is almost incomprehensible that the Bible teaches us that we are being transformed into the image of His glory! It is a work that the Spirit is already doing in us now, and one day, our body will also be transformed into a glorified body in the blink of an eye.

The Holy Spirit uses this word again in Romans 12:2:

*And do not be conformed to this world, but be **transformed** by the renewing of your mind, that you may prove what is that good and acceptable and perfect will of God.*

Our soul, that is to say, our mind, our will, and our emotions, also undergo that inner metamorphosis. As a result, we become that reflection of the glory of God more and more. We become a glorious Church existing out of believers who are full of God's glory and shine His light in the world around them. What a great plan of our Master Architect!

4

THE GLORIOUS CHURCH IS UNITED

In the previous chapters, we looked at passages from both the Old and New Testaments in which a group of people came together in unison, and God's glory filled the room. First, in the temple of Solomon, where a hundred and twenty priests came together and made a sound of praise in unison. Then, in Acts, where in the upper room on the day of Pentecost a hundred and twenty came together in unison, when suddenly the Holy Spirit filled each of them. In our search for a glorious Church, we cannot skip over this element. They came together in unison, and there was unity! Unity attracts the presence of God like a magnet.

Not only do the events above prove the importance that God places on unity, but also the following passages of Scripture, again one from the Old Testament and one from the New Testament, show very clearly how the Father loves when His children are one in Him and interact with each other in harmony. Where there is unity, the Lord commands His blessing! With these words, Psalm 133 ends, a Psalm that still knows how to touch our hearts centuries later.

Maybe it is because these words show the Father's heart for His household, His Children!

> *Behold, how good and how pleasant it is*
> *For brethren to dwell together in unity!*
> *It is like the precious oil upon the head,*
> *Running down on the beard,*
> *The beard of Aaron,*
> *Running down on the edge of his garments.*
> *It is like the dew of Hermon,*
> *Descending upon the mountains of Zion;*
> *For there the Lord commanded the blessing—*
> *Life forevermore.*
>
> — PSALM 133

I wonder if Jesus, our High Priest, thought of these words when He passionately prayed for unity. His prayer, which we know as the High Priestly prayer, is found in John 17. In the verses below, we read how eagerly Jesus desired that we would be one, one with Him, as He and the Father are perfectly one.

> *Holy Father, keep through Your name those whom You have given Me, that they may be one as We are.*
>
> — JOHN 17:11

> *I do not pray for these alone, but also for those who will believe in Me through their word; that they all may be one, as You, Father, are in Me, and I in You; that they also may be*

> *one in Us, that the world may believe that You sent Me.*
>
> —JOHN 17: 20, 21

> *And the glory which You gave Me I have given them, that they may be one just as We are one: I in them, and You in Me; that they may be made perfect in one, and that the world may know that You have sent Me and have loved them as You have loved Me.*
>
> —JOHN 17: 22, 23

If unity is so important to God, and He gets attracted by it, then that is a big reason to look deeper into that subject. Let us look at what the apostle Paul wrote about unity to the church in Corinth:

> *Now I plead with you, brethren, by the name of our Lord Jesus Christ, that you all speak the same thing, and that there be no divisions among you, but that you be **joined together** in the same mind and in the same judgment.*
>
> —1 CORINTHIANS 1:10

Spiritual Gifts Are Not a Sign of Spiritual Maturity

The church in Corinth was a church that did not lack any spiritual gift; all the gifts of the Spirit functioned in that church. There was a lot of the Holy Spirit visible in their meetings. They were rich in all aspects: in their speaking, knowledge, and power of God. This was, simply put, a very blessed church. But you can feel it coming; there was a but! BUT at the same time, they were also "terribly fleshly."

> *And I, brethren, could not speak to you as to spiritual people but as to carnal, as to babes in Christ. I fed you with milk and not with solid food; for until now you were not able to receive it, and even now you are still not able; for you are still carnal. For where there are envy, strife, and divisions among you, are you not carnal and behaving like mere men?*
>
> — 1 CORINTHIANS 3:1-3

Paul corrects them with strong words. He tells them plainly and simply that they are not at all as spiritual as they themselves think. He is essentially saying: Yes, you can prophesy greatly, but in your behavior, you are still carnal. You are actually still spiritual babies because you walk like natural people and do not show the behavior that is expected of a spiritual person.

Why such a rebuke? Why was Paul so strict? Simply because of the fights, the envy, and the divide in the church. Gently said, unity was hard to find. What tone would Paul raise against us? Would he be happy with the level of unity among the Christians in this country? To what extent do we show a different picture than the church in Corinth? The Bible holds up a mirror to us in that regard as well!

The Glorious Church Is in Unison

One in heart, one in vision, one in desire: one in Jesus! Let us let the words of Jesus sink in on us once again:

*I do not ask for these only, but also for those who will believe in me through their word, that they may all be one, just as you, Father, are in me, and I in you, that they also may be in us, **so that the world may believe** that you have sent me. The glory that you have given me I have given to them, **THAT THEY MAY BE ONE even as we are one**.*

The Church will remain the laughingstock of the world as long as she is divided. Of course, I do not mean that we should strive to ensure that every church worldwide will belong to the same denomination. That is not what it is about! **You cannot organize unity!** I am speaking about spiritual unity, unity on the micro level in our local churches, and unity on the macro level, unity among churches. There can be enormous variety and diversity as long as we keep the unity in Christ. You cannot organize unity; it is a case of the heart, a spiritual principle. It is worked by the Holy Spirit if we keep our hearts open for it. Paul wrote about the importance of unity to the church in Philippi and also to the church in Ephesus. Unity has everything to do with the maturity of the church and our credibility toward the outside world.

> *Conduct yourselves in a manner worthy of the gospel of Christ. Then I will know that you stand firm in the one Spirit, striving together as one for the faith of the gospel.*
>
> — PHILIPPIANS 1:27 (NIV - *SIMPLIFIED*)

> *...till we all come to the unity of the faith.*
>
> — EPHESIANS 4:13

The only unity is the unity of the faith—we are one by our faith that Jesus Christ is the Son of God, who died for our sins, is buried, is raised from the dead, and is sitting at the right hand of God. A good guideline for this is: "In essentials unity, in non-essentials liberty, and in all things, charity." Having said that, let us stop bickering about non-essentials, "Keep the main thing the main thing." We are called to win the world for Christ together, and with that perspective, we cannot afford to argue about small, unimportant things. We are called to interact with each other in love and unanimously go after the purposes of God.

Jan Sjoerd Pasterkamp

In November 2019, Jan Sjoerd Pasterkamp, a well-known and loved man of God in our country, was a guest at our Bible school. I had gotten to know him personally not long before that moment. A few months later, he transitioned to eternity, but what a blessing he has been to me in that short period. Rarely do you meet people who are so powerful and yet so gentle! That was what Jan Sjoerd was to me: gentle and courageous, powerful yet tender, with a strong backbone, and simultaneously so humble. I have enjoyed seeing that in him; with that, he has become a great example to me: something to follow myself and give to others.

With that in mind, I invited him to teach at RBI, our Bible school. How he enjoyed teaching all those young people who were so hungry to receive the Word. What a blessing that I got the opportunity to honor him that night. Jan Sjoerd spoke about many beautiful things that night, but one thing stuck with me, and I have never forgotten. He told about when he was on the mission field with his wife in Papua New Guinea, and they were reaching out for breakthroughs. One night, he saw an awfully ugly mask that moved in front of his window in the dark. In the natural, it was quite terrifying. But in the spirit, he rebuked and took authority over it. When he did that, the mask disappeared, and he heard the Lord say that this was an illustration of the spiritual stronghold over that country, witchcraft. Now that he knew who his primary enemy was, he could pray very specifically against it, and he saw great breakthroughs in that country. During their return to the Netherlands, he asked the Lord in the airplane what the spiritual stronghold was over the Netherlands. It is good to know what you are battling against. We are often busy with combatting the fruits, but if we know what the root is, we can be much more effective. If we want to see long-lasting breakthroughs in this country, the root will need to be addressed.

The Lord gave Jan Sjoerd the answer to his question. God let him know that the spiritual stronghold over the Netherlands is division.

"The spiritual stronghold over the Netherlands is division."

The word that Jan Sjoerd received that day is more current than ever. What a polarization we see in these times and if we do not watch out, it will also sneak into our churches. An old tactic of the enemy is: "divide and conquer." He knows that if he is able to spread division in the house of God, the house will not be able to stand.

On that night in November, Jan Sjoerd gave us the key for a breakthrough: *"To see a breakthrough, we need to work in the **opposite spirit**. That is the spiritual war we should fight. In this situation, the opposite spirit of division is **honor**. For many, that still is too big of a step, but we can start with at least showing **respect** to each other."*

We Break the Force of Division by Embracing a Culture of Honor

This is so important; we cannot underestimate this. How many church splits have there been in the Netherlands already, even in our time? How many fights have there been between leaders of this country? Fights that still leave their marks! How much disagreement does there still take place in local leadership teams? What is wrong? Do we have such bad leaders here? Is that the reason? Are we not capable of producing good leaders in the Netherlands? Or is something wrong with our church culture that causes leaders, churches, and ministries to not bloom as God wants them to? I am convinced that our church culture is the reason. We have let in the worldly spirit of division and let him do his work unhindered. That has left a trail of devastation behind: from church splits, discouraged leaders, and lost sheep.

This needs to change! The reality is that there are no perfect churches, and perfect leaders do not exist. The perfect person does not exist because "perfect people" do not exist. If perfect people do not exist, then we cannot expect leaders to be perfect. All of us, with no exceptions, are still a "work in progress." **The construction scaffolding of the Holy Spirit is around our lives, and He is still busy with His repair work.** The one is already further along than the other, but nobody is already perfect of himself. Thank God we are in Christ; the Father can see the end result from the beginning.

But while we are here on earth, we all have to deal with imperfections in ourselves and others.

That will be the case until Jesus comes back, and until then, we have to live according to the command to love others as ourselves. Jesus commanded us to love, and according to the law of love, we will be judged. The critical spirit does not belong in our churches. The spirit of *but I think*, of opinions and unhealthy discussions cannot have a voice in our churches any longer. Many Christians have the misconception that the church is a form of democracy. That is not what the Bible teaches us. We are part of a Kingdom in which Jesus is the King. The Church is part of that Kingdom, and Jesus Himself has put a structure in place for the Church of servant leadership.

Furthermore, He has given gifts to His Church, and those gifts are people who operate in what we have come to call *the fivefold ministry*. These are apostles, prophets, evangelists, pastors, and teachers. These people are gifts of Jesus to the church so that we can grow up to become mature Christians who make a difference in this world. In the Netherlands, Christians do not always treat the people Jesus offers as gifts respectfully. But even if the package does not please us, they are still gifts of Jesus. How we treat each other, our leaders, and the people in the ministry has everything to do with having a culture of honor. If we, as Christians, learn to honor our leaders and respect people with a ministry, then we operate in a spirit of honor, and with that, break the spirit of division over our country. If we receive people as sent of Christ, we will experience the revival that we have been longing for in prayer for centuries. But if we keep shooting down the messengers and ministries that Christ has given to us as a Church, then the Lord cannot give a breakthrough in this country.

In 2017, Jacky and I had the privilege of organizing Holland Ablaze, a conference of five days and nine powerful meetings, in which people from thirty-three countries from the entire world were represented. In total, more than three thousand people came to Holland Ablaze. Pastor Rodney Howard-Browne was the speaker, and on Thursday night, he gave a prophetic word for the Church in the Netherlands. He himself said that it was a word that he had never given in all his years of ministry. The atmosphere was loaded with the power of God when he spoke these words. It was a very important moment in the time for the Church in this country. I have known pastor Rodney for years and have been in hundreds of his meetings, and I can testify that this was a very specific and unique word for the Netherlands.

> *The Spirit of God said that all ministries we need for revival in the Netherlands are already available in our country, and if we receive those men and women for who they are in the spirit, we will see more revival than we can handle.*

A Culture of Honor

If we want to experience a national revival together, then that is the challenge we are facing: creating a culture of honor. Even Jesus could not do anything if He was not received and honored. At the beginning of His ministry, He went to Nazareth at one point, the city where He had lived from His young years, went to school, learned carpentry from His stepfather Joseph, and worked until He was thirty years old. Of course, He also wanted to teach about the Kingdom of God, heal sick people, and deliver bound people there. However, this was the only place in His years of ministry on earth where He COULD NOT do miracles. Is that not almost unbelievable? What was the reason for that? There was only one reason. His fellow villagers took offense at Him. They did not give Him the honor that He deserved.

> *Is this not the carpenter, the Son of Mary, and brother of James, Joses, Judas, and Simon? And are not His sisters here with us?" So they were offended at Him.*
>
> *But Jesus said to them, "A prophet is not without honor except in his own country, among his own relatives, and in his own house." Now He could do no mighty work there, except that He laid His hands on a few sick people and healed them. And He marveled because of their unbelief.*
>
> — MARK 6:3-6

A lack of honor cut the supply of God's power off. He COULD NOT do any works. He wanted to but could not because of their unbelief. What was the reason for that unbelief in Nazareth? They saw Him as a regular man, an equal, and took offense at Him, "Who does He think that He is?" They were not able to look through the package and see the gift that Jesus was, which is why they did not want to receive Him.

"The lack of honor cuts the supply of God's power off."

We have to keep in mind that Jesus had not appointed Himself as man of God but had received His ministry from heaven. That happened after His baptism in the Jordan River, when the Holy

Spirit landed on Him like a dove, and the voice of God sounded from heaven, "This is my beloved son, with whom I am well pleased." He had not appointed Himself, as we sometimes see people do. He was not a self-appointed prophet; He had not made a Facebook profile as "Apostle so-and-so"! He was appointed by God the Father Himself, blessed, and sent out. Men and women of God who have confirmed ministries, meaning they have been recognized and acknowledged as such, must be received as sent by God. Jesus still appoints ministries that are a gift to the Body!

> *And He Himself gave some to be apostles, some prophets, some evangelists, and some pastors and teachers, for the equipping of the saints for the work of ministry, for the edifying of the body of Christ, till we all come to the unity of the faith and of the knowledge of the Son of God, to a perfect man...*
>
> — EPHESIANS 4:11-13

Jesus gives the fivefold ministry to us to equip us so that we can attain maturity. Nobody can fully reach their destiny without those gifts. It is up to each one of us to find those gifts and receive them with honor and respect. By taking offense at them or holding them in low esteem, you sell yourself short! Each of them has received something from heaven to bless you with. Honor and appreciate that!

In the Netherlands, more and more is spoken about the culture of honor. We must articulate the essence of it properly in our teaching. Of course, honoring God comes in the first place. The Bible also speaks of treating each person honorably. Whether in society or the church, we are supposed to treat each other honorably. Unfortunately, the importance of honoring leaders appointed by God is still too often forgotten in *our churches*.

Remarkably, the first commandment that God connected to a promise is about honoring your parents: "Honor your father and your mother, that your days may be long upon the land which the Lord your God is giving you" (Ex. 20:12). In the New Testament, this is confirmed once more in Ephesians 6:2-3. Honor is something you initially give to the authority placed *above* you. That not only means to God in the first place but also to your parents, your spiritual leaders, and your employer. That is often hard for a Dutch person. We like talking about a *culture of honor*, but in practice, we find it quite hard to walk in that. I believe this stems from our desire to distribute everything evenly; we like to have leveling. Preferably, we do not want to see any outliers. We find it hard when somebody stands out from the crowd. Everyone needs to be a little bit the same, "act normally, then you already act crazy enough" is a Dutch motto. But that is not a mindset we can find in the Bible! There are certain things we should distribute fairly. We may give with our finances to the less well-off, and we may appreciate the unseen parts of the Body and put the people who are busy behind the scenes into the spotlight. That is all very important and biblical, but the Bible does not teach about equal distribution in every area.

Jesus told the parable of the talents, in which not everyone received equally: one person received five talents, the other two, and another one. Everyone received according to their own capability. Equal distribution was not the case, but the Lord distributed as He pleased. Our *sense of justice* may say, "That is not fair, Lord!" But it is not up to us to discuss this with Him. The Lord makes it clear that we should be thankful for what He entrusts us with, whether it is a lot or a little in our eyes. With a grateful heart, we can work with what He has given us. The person who had received the one talent did nothing with it. His talent was taken away and given to the person who went to work with his five talents and doubled what was entrusted to him. A wise lesson for us to learn!

> *For to everyone who has, more will be given, and he will have abundance; but from him who does not have, even what he has will be taken away.*
>
> — MATTHEW 25:29

If we are good stewards of what is entrusted to us, we will be blessed with a larger area. Who is faithful in the little, more will be entrusted to them. But whoever is not faithful will see his area get smaller. That is the economy of the Kingdom.

Two things often get mixed up. YES, we are all equal in the Kingdom in the sense that we are all saved by grace. God loves each one of us, and we are brothers and sisters in His family. But NO, we are not all equal in position. God calls some of us to the fivefold ministry; others are deacons or elders, but not everyone is placed in a leadership position. There are differences in calling, gifts, talents, and the place we take in His Kingdom. We should not try to play God by lowering outliers or stipulating ourselves over who is allowed to take that place. We should not want to secure a place for ourselves that God does not have in mind for us, either. He is the one who gives the promotion. If He does not promote you or certain people, why are you trying to? If God has appointed a leader and anointed them, who are you to lower that person? It is time that we stop being afraid of leadership and authority in the church. God says that people who lead well are worthy of receiving the honor, "Let the elders who rule well be counted worthy of double honor, especially those who labor in the word and doctrine" (1 Tim. 5:17 NKJV). Here, the Bible speaks about more than appreciating leaders but encourages us to give a double portion of honor to those who lead well and preach the Word. We should give that honor generously to the people here in the Netherlands from the fivefold ministry who preach and teach!

If we want to be a glorious church, we should receive the people Jesus gives us with open arms. We should celebrate and honor them as people sent by God to enrich our lives. Let this chapter challenge you to appreciate and respect your pastors and leaders. Serve the vision God has given them with your whole heart. Express your gratitude for all their efforts and for how they are investing in your life and those of others. Bless them and let your appreciation not only be heard but let it also be known by taking them out for dinner once or giving them a gift, anything that the Lord may put in your heart. Let them know how your life has changed by their preaching and what they live out by example. And for those who read this and do not know the culture within our congregation, I am not writing this to get something for myself. God has blessed us enormously with a very positive and hungry group of people who pull out everything God has put into us as leaders.

"Make it joyful for your leaders to lead you."

If we develop that culture of honor toward leaders and each other, we will grow to the unity of the faith and maturity in Christ together. Where that unity is, God commands His blessing! We have seen that in Psalm 133. How great it will be to live in that area of complete blessing of God together. If I think about that, my heart gets attracted to it like a magnet. I want to be there! You too?

> *Behold, how good and how pleasant it is for brethren to dwell together in unity! For there the Lord commanded the blessing.*
>
> — PSALM 133:1,3

How lovely is it to start tasting what it means to be there! We interact with each other in unity and appreciation. What great joy! This also gives us a strong sound outward because the world can taste if there is harmony and love somewhere. Again, a house that is divided against itself cannot stand. But if mutual love and a culture of honor determine the environment in the church, then we will become so attractive in a world where lovelessness and polarization seem to get the upper hand more and more.

5

THE GLORIOUS CHURCH OVERCOMES

I believe we have entered a time of overwhelming victory as the Church of Jesus Christ.

> *Arise, shine; For your light has come! And the glory of the Lord is risen upon you. For behold, the darkness shall cover the earth, and deep darkness the people; but the Lord will arise over you, and His glory will be seen upon you. The Gentiles shall come to your light, and kings to the brightness of your rising.*
>
> —ISAIAH 60:1-3

The Bible is clear about the fact that darkness will increase in the last days. We see it happen more and more, even recently, that the darkness seems to cover the earth at an accelerated tempo. It seems as though a veil has covered this generation so that what is straight is called crooked, and what is crooked is called straight. Sometimes, I read the news and shake my head because of how unbelievable it is that injustice that was impossible to be acceptable just ten years ago seems to be accepted now. Now, we can observe that and sit by and watch it happen, hoping and praying that Jesus comes to get us out of this dark world quickly. But I do not read my Bible like that.

If I read in this passage that darkness will cover the earth and thick darkness the people, I do not stop reading there because the Bible continues: *but the Lord will arise* **over you**, *and His glory will be seen upon you!*

God does not only let us know what will happen on the earth, but He also encourages His children at the same time! He is essentially saying: But you are different than the world! What applies to the world does not apply to you! We see an encouraging example of this in the Bible. When the people of Israel lived in slavery for generations in Egypt, God called Moses to lead His people out with signs and wonders. One day, complete darkness covered the land of Egypt on a word of God, except for in Goshen, where the Israelites lived; there it remained light.

> *So Moses stretched out his hand toward heaven, and there was thick darkness in all the land of Egypt three days. They did not see one another; nor did anyone rise from his place for three days. But all the children of Israel had light in their dwellings.*
>
> — EXODUS 10:22, 23

GOD SAYS about us in His Word, "You are completely different, you have gotten to know Christ" (Ephesians 4:20). We need to be aware that we are in the world but not of the world. We are here as ambassadors and representatives of a heavenly Kingdom. The earth is not our home. In these last days, God will make the difference between the righteous and the unrighteous visible. This must be printed in our hearts so that we do not get carried away with the stream of this world. We walk in the light; they in the darkness. We have life; they do not have life yet. We are not overcome by the world; we have overcome the world through Christ.

> *For whatever is born of God overcomes the world. And this is the victory that has overcome the world—our faith.*
>
> — 1 JOHN 5:4

Some people always experience that they are in a fight. I do not believe that the Bible teaches this. **Christ has fought the fight for us and has overcome.** The only fight we need to fight is the fight of faith. Jesus disarmed the rulers and authorities and put them to open shame by triumphing over them (Col. 2:15). We can rest in His completed work and, out of that rest, remain standing in every battle in the reality of His victory.

> *For we do not wrestle against flesh and blood, but against principalities, against powers, against the rulers of the darkness of this age, against spiritual hosts of wickedness in the heavenly places. Therefore take up the whole armor of God, that you may be able to with-*

> *stand in the evil day, and having done all, to stand. Stand therefore.*
>
> — EPHESIANS 6:12-14

People read these verses and make a big thing out of spiritual battle. Spiritual battle is a reality, but how you approach it decides the outcome. The Bible teaches us that there is a constant battle going on, but God has given us the weapons to stand and to remain standing in our position as overcomers. After having done everything, stand. His strategy is that we continue to stand right through the struggle, the obstacles, and the opposition! Remain standing in your position of righteousness, your position of the son of God, your position of loved one, your position of healing, and your position of freedom. Remain standing! It does not say: fight against the devil. No, it says: remain standing in the faith that Jesus has won the battle! If you constantly focus on the devil and the fight, it will be hard to live the overflowing life of Christ. However, if you focus on Jesus, His victory on the cross, His position in the heavenly realms, and your position in Him, you will walk in joy! The good news is that when you have joy, you have power. Let us, therefore, keep our eyes focused on Jesus, who fought the fight for us and came out as the Conqueror. He has, as a result, acquired all power in heaven and on earth, and He sits at the right hand of God in the heavenly realms, and we sit there with Him.

> *Yet in all these things we are more than conquerors through Him who loved us.*
>
> — ROMANS 8:37

In all this, we are not just conquerors; we are more than conquerors! This means Jesus has won the fight, and we can enjoy the benefits of His victory. You could compare this with a top-level boxer who goes into the ring for a fight for the title. He fights his way through twelve rounds, catching the heavy blows, and fights himself until he is bloodied to victory. In the last round, he knocks his opponent to the ground. His fists go into the air, as he is now the champion in his weight class. What a victory! The title is paired with an enormous cash bonus in the form of a big check. With a bloody face, muscles aching, and completely exhausted, the conqueror comes home with his check of millions. When he arrives home, his wife opens the door, and with open arms and a big smile, she welcomes her champion and their big fat check! She herself has not lifted a finger and did not catch a blow, but she does reap the benefits of the victory that her husband has achieved. She is MORE than a conqueror! This paints a nice picture of us in Christ. He has fought the fight, but we, His beloved Bride, share in the victory. By His victory, we are saved, and by His stripes, we are healed. And because He became poor for us, we have become rich in Him! What a grace! We are more than conquerors in Him!

A verse that I personally find very helpful is Proverbs 4:18:

But the path of the just is like the shining sun, that shines ever brighter unto the perfect day.

Our path is not from the mountaintop into the valley to struggle for years until we reach another little hilltop. No, our path is a path that only goes up and never goes down. Our path is upward! In Christ, we are righteous, and the Bible shows us that the path of the righteous shines ever brighter. We are not dependent on the current economy or at the mercy of whoever sits in the little tower in the Hague. We are connected to Him sitting on the throne, and He still rules today! In faith, we can say that regardless of how dark it may get in this world, our path will remain lit. We go from victory to victory in faith.

John Osteen, the father of Joel Osteen, was a great man of faith. He was the one who started Lakewood Church with a handful of people in a small steel building in Houston and saw the church grow to what was the largest church in the US at the time with eighteen thousand people. John Osteen told a story that touched me deeply.

There was a time in his life when he was battling fear a lot. He did not dare fly anymore and was scared to travel, and that fear created an obstacle for him to walk in his calling. As a man of God, it was a tough dilemma. But it was his reality, and he did not know how to get out of that prison of fear. One day, he had a dream or vision in which he saw the devil walk up to him with a threatening look. John Osteen was paralyzed by fear and did not know what to do, but in his fear, he called on the name of Jesus. All of a sudden, Jesus was there between him and the devil. He sighed a breath of relief and thought to himself: Great, Jesus is here. He will take on the devil for me. But to his surprise, Jesus started walking backward, away from the devil and toward John. "You are going the wrong way, Lord," John Osteen cried. "You need to walk toward the devil to drive him away!" Jesus, however, kept walking backward with slow steps, and then the following happened. When Jesus got to him, he saw that Jesus took another step backward with His right leg and went into John's own right leg. Then, Jesus put His right arm back, and it went into John's right arm. Then, Jesus put His left arm into John's left arm, and last of all, He put His left foot into John's left foot, and suddenly, Jesus had completely disappeared into John. The moment he saw this happen, the revelation came to John like a bomb: Christ IN ME, the hope of glory! With that fresh revelation in his heart, he looked at the devil who still stood in the same place, pointed his finger at him, and commanded him to leave in the name of Jesus. Immediately, the devil disappeared, and with him, all fear also disappeared. John was a revelation richer: Jesus lives in me. He moves through me and exercises His authority through me.

What a revelation! I wonder what the world would look like if we all had that revelation. We would beg less and command more. We would be less likely to end up in a victim mentality and speak and act more from the mentality of an overcomer. We would think less of all our own needs and carry out God's power more to a world in need.

> *Now thanks be to God who always leads us in triumph in Christ, and through us diffuses the fragrance of His knowledge in every place.*
>
> — 2 CORINTHIANS 2:14

In Christ, we always have the victory. This sometimes seems hard to believe when we are in the middle of a situation and do not see the victory yet. Then, our feelings and thoughts sometimes yell louder than the Word of God. It is then especially necessary to focus on the truth of God's Word and hold onto that truth. The Bible says that we walk by faith, not by sight (2 Cor. 5:7). It shows that faith and sight are opposites. If we live by what we see with our natural senses (sight), we will lose the battle. But if we live by faith, then we have the victory. That is the fight of faith. It is the fight to stay in faith and not listen to what our senses tell us. Peter received this lesson in person.

Immediately Jesus made His disciples get into the boat and go before Him to the other side, while He sent the multitudes away. And when He had sent the multitudes away, He went up on the mountain by Himself to pray. Now when evening came, He was alone there. But the boat was now in the middle of the sea, tossed by the waves, for the wind was contrary. Now in the fourth watch of the night Jesus went to them, walking on the sea. And when the disciples saw Him walking on the sea, they were troubled, saying, "It is a ghost!" And they cried out for fear. But immediately Jesus spoke to them, saying, "Be of good cheer! It is I; do not be afraid." And Peter answered Him and said, "Lord, if it is You, command me to come to You on the water." So He said, "Come." And when Peter had come down out of the boat, he walked on the water to go to Jesus. But when he saw that the wind was boisterous, he was afraid; and beginning to sink he cried out, saying, "Lord, save me!" And immediately Jesus stretched out His hand and caught him, and said to him, "O you of little faith, why did you doubt?" And when they got into the boat, the wind ceased.

— MATTHEW 14:22-32

"Make it joyful for your leaders to lead you."

So many lessons can be taken away from this story, but let us zoom in on Peter. He was an experienced fisherman who knew about the lake and the treacherous winds that sometimes blew. He had, without a doubt, experienced storms before. With the other disciples, he is sitting in the boat when a strong headwind arises, and the situation becomes more and more threatening. Jesus had sent them out before Him, so He is not there to help them, or, at least, in their perception, that is the reality. In the fourth watch of the night, Jesus comes toward them, walking over the waves of the sea. In that time, everyone knew about the four night watches, the different time blocks in which the night was divided. Jesus came in the fourth watch of the night, which means in the final hours before the night ended and the new morning would dawn. Why did He come so late when they were struggling for so long already? In our perception, that is on the late side. But God is always on time. Just like the disciples, we can learn to trust His timing. He always sees us, also in our need, and comes to help us in His time.

They see a figure approaching over the waves and scream with fear, presuming it to be a ghost. But when Jesus says, "It is I, do not fear," Peter responds immediately as usual, "If it is You, command me to come to you over the water." Jesus answers with one simple word, "Come." On that word, Peter climbs out of the boat, and he starts walking on the water. Miraculously, what an act of faith! In a sense, you could say that Peter was not walking on the water but on the Word. The Word of God is a solid foundation, even if the ground underneath you seems to sink. In the same way that Peter walked on the Word, you and I can also put our full weight of trust on the Word of God. If He says it, then it is so.

> *God is not a man, that He should lie, nor a son of man, that He should repent. Has He said, and will He not do? Or has He spoken, and will He not make it good?*
>
> — NUMBERS 23:19

"Faith is acting on the Word of God."

Faith is acting on the Word of God. It is acting in faith that the Word of God is true, even if your circumstances seem to say the opposite. It is a lot easier to agree with that in theory than to walk that out in the practice of your life. Peter also faced this test because, during this unusual night walk on the water, there was a moment in which his eyes wandered from Jesus and focused on the waves. In that moment, he went from walking in faith to walking by sight. His senses took over. He heard the storm and felt the power of the wind. His eyes saw how high the waves were, and the fear took him over: I must be crazy. Why did I step out of that peaceful boat? This is not normal. At that moment, he sank down and called, "Lord, save me!" Thank God, what happened then is good news for us all! In the midst of his need, grace got a face, the face of Jesus, who stretched out His strong hand and grabbed him. By the hand of Jesus, Peter walked back to the boat. He did get rebuked by the Lord for his unbelief. Imagine you've just been the first human being to walk on water, not counting Jesus, and you get a slap on the wrist because your faith is too small! The reason was, of course, that a mistake was made that many after Peter would also still make. You and I have probably put our sensory perception above the Word of God, as well. We do not do that consciously, but unconsciously, we put our truth above God's truth. We live as if our perception of reality is a higher reality than God's Word. We are not always aware of how much God longs that we learn to walk in childlike faith.

> *By faith we understand that the worlds were framed by the word of God, so that the things which are seen were not made of things which are visible.*
>
> — HEBREWS 11:3

The Bible teaches us that the Word of God has created everything that is visible, tangible, and perceivable. Everything that we can perceive with our senses in the natural exists because of the Word that God spoke during creation. Which reality is larger, the one that is created or the One that created it, being the Word? Obviously, the latter. In other words, we should understand that the Word is a larger reality than what our senses perceive, and we can trust that the creating Word of God still has the power today to change situations. God's Word is more real, more solid, and more steady ground than any earthly assurance! In Peter's situation, the one word that Jesus spoke, "Come," was stronger and mightier than the natural laws of gravity, stronger than the waves, and stronger than the stormy wind. All those natural things had to bow to the Word of God. It was up to Peter to believe in that Word and remain focused on the Lord who had spoken it rather than letting himself be frightened by the natural conditions. For us, the challenge is not any different!

Let us look at another example in the Bible. In Acts 27 and 28, we read about Paul, who is aboard a ship as a prisoner on his way to Rome to stand trial before the emperor. The ship got caught in a heavy storm, which Paul had already warned about. It was so bad that the crew had to lower the sails and, with that, hand the ship over to the wind. In the following days, the cargo and the ship's gear were thrown overboard.

To make matters worse, it was pitch black, and almost no food was left. After floating back and forth on the sea for two weeks, they saw land and headed toward it. The ship ran aground on something close to the beach and broke into pieces. The crew, the soldiers, and all the prisoners had to go into the water to swim to shore if they could. Others reached the beach by holding onto debris from the ship. Once they arrived on land, it appeared they had reached the island of Malta. The islanders had pity on them and started a fire so that they could warm themselves. Paul helped and gathered some branches for the fire, but when he threw a bundle on the fire, a snake came out because of the heat and bit into his hand. The inhabitants of the island observed this and said, "This man is cursed. He survived the shipwreck, and now, he will be killed by a snake." Paul, however, did something very simple in which we can learn something. He shook the snake off in the fire and continued as if nothing happened, or rather, he gave the enemy no attention and continued moving in faith. Translated to the situations we sometimes experience, you could say: He shook off discouragement, somber thoughts, feelings of despair, thoughts of giving up, or the negative words of other people and remained standing in what God called him to. When the inhabitants of the island saw that Paul had not suffered any damage from the snake bite, their opinion of him changed. Now, they did not view him as a cursed criminal, but they were convinced he was a god.

On that island where Paul had suffered a shipwreck as a prisoner, he suddenly got treated as a prince. In this day and age, we would say that he was offered free accommodation in the best Airbnb in Malta. This is because he was invited to stay at the estate of the leading man of the Island, *Publius*. The father of Publius appeared to be quite sick in bed, but after Paul had prayed, he laid hands on him and healed him. That news spread over the island quickly, and the others who were sick came to Paul and got healed. Paul was overloaded with tributes of honor, and when the group was ready to head out to sail, everything they needed to make the trip to Rome was provided for. Wow, what an illustration is painted here. You can call that coming out of the battle as a victor!

We all get into situations in which that ugly snake tries to bite us. It can happen suddenly, and for weeks, you have experienced all sorts of misery. You just got through it, and out of the blue, you still get bitten at an unexpected moment. That is how it was with Paul. What we can learn from this story is that it can be a trap to "fight the spiritual battle." Paul did not even pray for the snakebite. He shook off the snake "as if nothing was wrong." **You and I may also shake off the lies of the enemy and not pay any attention, either.** We can trust in the fact that He, who has started a good work in us, will surely complete it.

Every good word He has spoken over you, He will establish. Not one of the promises He has spoken over you will remain unfulfilled. It will happen! It is up to us to simply keep believing and hold onto it.

It says in Isaiah 60:7: "and I will beautify my beautiful house."

The New Living Translation says it like this: "and I will make my Temple glorious."

God is ready to glorify His Church, show the difference between righteous and unrighteous, and do mighty deeds with His strong hand. Especially now that the darkness is increasing, His light will shine through us stronger.

There will definitely be opposition to that. We should not be surprised by that. Jesus said, "'A servant is not greater than his master.' If they persecuted Me, they will also persecute you" (John 15:20). But Jesus also said:

> *And on this rock I will build My church, and the gates of Hades shall not prevail against it.*
>
> — MATTHEW 16:18

His Church will not be overwhelmed by the attacks of the kingdom of darkness. His Church will grow in esteem and become stronger and stronger, and when Jesus comes back to get His Bride, He will come for a glorious, overcoming, radiating Church!

AFTERWORD

The End Times Church

We have looked at all kinds of elements of the Glorious Church, and hopefully, this has set a fire in you to be part of that pure, radiating, overcoming Church that impacts this world. Everything the Bible shows us about the Church in the end times is to build us up and make us ready. But ultimately, it is the Holy Spirit who will make the Word living in our hearts. That is why I want to close this book by honoring the Holy Spirit for Who He is and what He does.

He is the One who came as a substitute for Jesus to be our Helper.

He helps us to take possession of every promise of God.

He is the One who changes us from the inside out and makes transformation happen.

He is the One who leads us in the full truth.

He is the One by whom we are sealed until that big day in which we look Jesus in the eyes.

He is the One who leads the Church and raises her up to maturity.

Forming and transforming the Church into the Glorious Church is the work of the Holy Spirit. Without the Holy Spirit, the local church is no more than a social club.

He brings the life, He brings the dynamic.

He initiates the supernatural aspect of being a church.

Without Him, the Church would be a lifeless organization without any form of impact.

It was the Holy Spirit in the book of Acts who ensured that things happened.

Most people refer to that book as *Acts of the Apostles*, but actually, we should call it *Acts of the Holy Spirit*. The apostles worked in submission to the Holy Spirit; they could do nothing without Him. Jesus had said it Himself, "Wait in Jerusalem until you receive the power of the Holy Spirit… Then you will be My witnesses!"

All aspects of the glorious Church discussed in this book are not workable by human programs. They are not meant to be reasoned or philosophized about; they are not organizable either. They must be born in people's hearts through revelation and the power of the Holy Spirit. That is hard for us because we like to keep control. Ideally, we would use a formula and keep the process under control, but God will not share His glory with people. He will do the work, and He will get the glory!

Fortunately, the Holy Spirit does not want to do it alone. He wants to work together with you and me.

Afterword

We are the vessels, He is the Treasure.

He is the Hand that moves, we are the glove to the Hand.

He is the Craftsman, we are the equipment.

Our task is to submit to Him so He can do His work! Before a meeting, I often pray, "Lord, I do not want to stand in the way; Do what You want to do."

Many people think that God will bring revival out of His sovereignty and at the time appointed by Him. But history shows us that revival comes when believers start to hunger and thirst for Him. Revival starts IN us, in you, and in me! It is not something that takes place outside somewhere and happens to blow into a church. Revival comes if a burning desire arises in believers who do not want to settle for "Christianity-light" anymore. Believers who do not want to drink "Jesus-zero," watered down, without flavor, without power. Believers who long for what the Bible shows us: salvation, healing, deliverance, movement, every day, every week, every year until Jesus comes back! When that hunger and that desire take over in us, then God moves. Reinhard Bonnke often said, "God moves with the people who are moving. He does not sit with the chair warmers." When we start moving, the Holy Spirit moves through us.

The Holy Spirit is not a feeling of goosebumps or some manifestation. He is a Person! He wants to speak, He wants to work, He wants to form, He wants to knead, and He wants all the space in His Church. But how much space does He get to do what He wants? When can He do what He wants to do? We should not keep the Holy Spirit outside of our church doors in order to not offend people. That is disrespectful to the Person of God, the Holy Spirit. Paul said, "For do I now persuade men, or God? Or do I seek to please men?

For if I still pleased men, I would not be a bondservant of Christ" (Galatians 1:10).

We need to have a good look in the mirror and ask ourselves who really is the boss. If it is us, it is our church. But if it is Him, it is His church, and the people are His sheep. If it is His church, then He will also build and protect it. But if it is our church... Then good luck. I am speaking from the heart now, "Let us give the Holy Spirit the full room! In our own lives, at our work, and in *our* churches." The moment I say this, all kinds of thoughts might come in: "Should we then cry, laugh, or roll on the ground for the whole meeting? Should we constantly pray in tongues or prophesy? Does it mean we now have to be very emotional and make a lot of noise? A hundred percent *no*! The image many have of the work of the Holy Spirit is that it can be a bit scary. Maybe you have been in meetings where things happened that you did not know if it was from God or not.

What we have to remember is that we do not throw out the baby with the bathwater. People do crazy things sometimes under the guise of the Holy Spirit. But that does not mean we should throw everything related to the Holy Spirit overboard. There are enough people who have abused money, but we all still use it every day. Similarly, many have abused the speed capabilities of their car and have created traffic accidents. But that does not stop us from stepping into the car to go to work or buy groceries.

This is also how it is with the work of the Holy Spirit. The Bible teaches us that all things should be done decently and in order (1 Corinthians 14:40). Firstly, it should be clear that something needs to be done. Secondly, the Bible teaches us that it must be done in order.

The question is then what God means by *in order*. We need to understand that God's order can look very different from what we understand under order. In God's order for the church, the Word has the highest place, and the Holy Spirit should be in charge. The Holy Spirit will never work outside of the boundaries of the Word. He wants to bring transformation in the lives of individual Christians, and at the same time, He will see to it that what happens is for the upbuilding of the church. Our best model is the New Testament. Everywhere Jesus came, great signs and wonders took place, great joy came, and lives were transformed. BUT roofs were also torn apart in the middle of a meeting, eyes were spit on, and demons left people with loud screeching while the preaching was still going on. That is God's good order! In Acts and the letters of Paul, we see the same pattern:

The disciples who came outside from the upper room seemed drunk.

The sick were laid on the streets of Jerusalem because if Peter walked there, his shadow healed them.

Philip turned a city upside down in such a way that in a bonfire of joy, all magic arts books with a very high value to them were burned.

Where Paul came, both revival and uproar broke loose.

Etcetera, etcetera, etcetera. All of this falls under the heading of *God's good order*. It creates a blueprint for the Church that we may follow.

In these last days, the Holy Spirit will do a mighty work on earth. The Church will arise in power and glory, and whole nations will be shaken.

See that you do not refuse Him who speaks. For if
they did not escape who refused Him who

> *spoke on earth, much more shall we not escape if we turn away from Him who speaks from heaven, whose voice then shook the earth; but now He has promised, saying, "Yet once more I shake not only the earth, but also heaven." Now this, "Yet once more," indicates the removal of those things that are being shaken, as of things that are made, that the things which cannot be shaken may remain. Therefore, since we are receiving a kingdom which cannot be shaken, let us have grace, by which we may serve God acceptably with reverence and godly fear. For our God is a consuming fire.*
>
> — HEBREWS 12:25-29

God spoke that He would shake everything once more. The writer of the letter, Hebrews, quotes the words of the prophet Haggai. We have already focused on that in chapter two and seen that Haggai prophesied during the rebuilding of the temple after the return of the people from Babylon. Immediately after Haggai's prophecy about the shaking of the nations, he spoke about the temple that would be filled with greater glory than the first temple. Of course, he did not speak about the temple they were rebuilding because that temple paled in comparison to the first temple that Solomon had built. No, he prophesied about the future temple that would be built by the Holy Spirit with spiritual stones. The future temple would consist of born-again believers and Jesus the Cornerstone. He prophesied about that spiritual temple that it would have an all-surpassing glory; he spoke about the glorious Church!

That glorious Church emerges during a time of great shaking. Everything that can be shaken will be shaken. That is why the Holy Spirit encourages us to be focused on the unshakable Kingdom we have received. In other words, our life should be built upon Jesus, our unshakeable foundation, and we should fill our lives with everything that has eternal value, and that is unshakable.

In this day and age, we see a lot of shaking and wavering, but we do not have to be worried about anything. I can say, in all honesty, that we experience peace in the midst of everything. This earth is not our home. We have a permanent house in heaven, in the house of our Father. Here, on earth, He will also protect us, supply for us, and abundantly give us the good things. If we see all things people put their trust in melt as wax before the sun, we can be at ease because we have a Refuge they do not know. We take refuge in the presence of God, where everything we need is found in abundance. Psalm 91 speaks about this, and we may know for sure that all these promises are for us because we are His beloved children.

> *He who dwells in the secret place of the Most High*
> *Shall abide under the shadow of the Almighty.*
> *I will say of the Lord, "He is my refuge and my fortress;*
> *My God, in Him I will trust."*
> *Surely He shall deliver you from the snare of the fowler*
> *And from the perilous pestilence.*
> *He shall cover you with His feathers,*
> *And under His wings you shall take refuge;*
> *His truth shall be your shield and buckler.*
> *You shall not be afraid of the terror by night,*

Nor of the arrow that flies by day,
Nor of the pestilence that walks in darkness,
Nor of the destruction that lays waste at noonday.
A thousand may fall at your side,
And ten thousand at your right hand;
But it shall not come near you.
Only with your eyes shall you look,
And see the reward of the wicked.
Because you have made the Lord, who is my refuge,
Even the Most High, your dwelling place,
No evil shall befall you,
Nor shall any plague come near your dwelling;
For He shall give His angels charge over you,
To keep you in all your ways.
In their hands they shall bear you up,
Lest you dash your foot against a stone.
You shall tread upon the lion and the cobra,
The young lion and the serpent you shall trample underfoot.

— PSALM 91:1-13

The words of this Psalm are so beautiful, words to read, re-read, and store in our hearts. You could personalize the words every time you read this Psalm so that the promises contained in it sink deeply into your heart. I want you to do that below with the verses that the Psalm ends with (verses 14-16). Read these words and believe that the Father speaks them very personally to you:

> "Because you have set his love upon Me,
>   therefore I will deliver you;
> I will set you on high, because you have
>   known My name.
> You shall call upon Me, and I will
>   answer you;
> I will be with you in trouble;
> I will deliver you and honor you.
> With long life I will satisfy you,
> And show you My salvation."

While we hold onto Him, live in Him, move and have our being, we will not be a sick, weak, feeble Church. No, on the contrary, the Church will be healthy and strong, a radiating reflection of Jesus in this world. Everything in this world, all the earthly things, will stumble. But we who are founded on the Rock Jesus Christ will remain standing. Whole crowds will come to us to get to know Jesus. Before Jesus comes back to get His Bride, the earth will experience a gigantic revival and be covered with the glory of God as the waters cover the sea. I believe that you and I will not only be part of it, but we will stand in the midst of it!

ABOUT THE AUTHOR

Shortly after Ben gave his life to Jesus, he moved to Tampa, Florida, to go to the Bible school connected to Rodney Howard-Browne's ministry. That is also where he met his wife, Jacky, and they married in 2010. Jacky had given her life to Jesus at 12 years old, and from an early age, she already had a desire to serve the Lord full-time. After serving faithfully for six years in different facets of the ministry, Ben and Jacky felt that God called them to start a church in the Netherlands: The River Amsterdam. With their daughter of almost a year, they moved to the Netherlands with a burning passion in their hearts to see people have an encounter with Jesus and to help them fully flourish in their God-given potential.

ABOUT THE RIVER AMSTERDAM

The River Amsterdam is a dynamic, growing church where both young and old find a home, meet God, and get equipped to make an impact on the world around them.

When Ben and Jacky moved to the Netherlands in 2013, they did not know anybody in the region of Amsterdam, but the vision of God burned in their hearts. They found a small sanctuary, did outreaches, and started with weekly meetings. Now, almost ten years later, they lead a vibrant congregation where people give their lives to Christ every week, receive a touch from God, and new leaders are formed. It is a place where people from all over the Netherlands come with joy to receive from the Lord.

If you would like to come take a look in the River on a Sunday or during one of the conferences, please go to **www.riveramsterdam.nl** for more information.

ABOUT RIVER BIBLE INSTITUTE
THE NETHERLANDS

In 2015, Ben and Jacky also started a Bible school where students from all over the Netherlands are trained to follow the call of God in their lives. It is a school where anointed teaching from the Word of God is central, and the Holy Spirit gets the room to work. RBI the Netherlands is not only focused on transferring knowledge but also is focused on helping the students to make a connection with their own lives. In short, the lessons are not only powerful but also practical, with the goal of seeing a transformation take place in the lives of the students.

RBI the Netherlands is recommended for people who feel a calling for a full-time ministry and for people who have a desire to grow in their walk with Jesus. Three years of teaching are offered within a total of 24 life-changing subjects that lift the faith of the students and their walk with God to a new level. From the start of RBI the Netherlands, all years of classes are offered practically free of charge. New students can enroll both in September and January. Go to bibleschool.nl for more information.

Support This Work

The mandate on the life of Ben and Jacky reaches further than only the River Amsterdam. When God called them to go to the Netherlands, He spoke the following words,

"The dams and dikes will break, and this land will flow with the knowledge of the glory of the Lord, like the water covers the sea."

To see that God-given vision fulfilled, Ben and Jacky, together with the different teams within the River Amsterdam, are constantly busy with this mission:

* Reach the lost

* Revive believers

* Raise up leaders

To help see this mission fulfilled, the River Foundation is established.

Through the River Foundation, there is the possibility to fulfill God's assignment on a greater scale in the Netherlands and beyond. This is being expressed by, among other things, sowing the Word through the Bible school, multimedia projects, and books like this one. In addition, evangelizing campaigns and weekends of Revival meetings are organized throughout the Netherlands and in Europe.

Perhaps you have been blessed by this book or one of our meetings or conferences and want to support this mission. You can then become a partner and help us reach even more people with the Gospel and the power of the Holy Spirit.

The monthly support of our partners helps us to fulfill the mission that God has given us. On **www.riverfoundation.eu**, you can read how you can become a partner.

www.ingramcontent.com/pod-product-compliance
Lightning Source LLC
LaVergne TN
LVHW051525070426
835507LV00023B/3310